THE
CHINESE
ZODIAC

A SERIOUSLY
SILLY GUIDE

ANITA MANGAN
WITH SARAH FORD

PORTICO

For Matt x

INTRODUCTION

You would think that Chinese astrology was easy. As the symbols used are animals, simply find your animal and Bob's your uncle; away you go. But hold your horses, there's way more to it than you might think – it's a complex science that can give a real insight into a person. However, in the interest of sanity, this book has kept it simple. Take a big chunk of Chinese wisdom, a small dose of science and sprinkle it with a bit of British humour and you have a recipe to stave off boredom for an hour or so, and a way to give your family and friends a fit of the giggles.

HOW DOES IT WORK?

It's all about time, with the moon, the sun and Jupiter all playing their part. The Chinese New Year is based upon the phases of the moon and can fall anytime between late January and the end of February. Your Chinese zodiac is based on your birth year and each year is represented by an animal. Each animal gets the spotlight once every 12 years.

WHY USE ANIMALS?

Once upon a time, so legend has it, the gods called all the animals to a celebration, but only 12 animals accepted. To thank them, the gods dedicated a year from the calendar to them. The order of the zodiac was determined by a race to the celebration. The Rat came first, apparently he hitched a ride with Ox but, as they neared the finish line, he jumped off and scurried ahead to beat Ox, so Ox came second. Last over the line was poor Pig, who supposedly overslept. The zodiac animals run in strict order of when they arrived at the celebration: Rat, Ox, Tiger, Rabbit, Dragon, Snake, Horse, Goat, Monkey, Rooster, Dog, and finally Pig. The Chinese believe that the animal that relates to your birth year will influence your personality, love life, career and your destiny.

Just pull up a comfy chair, put the kettle on and grab some loved ones to find out all you need to know.

CONTENTS

ZODIAC ANIMALS

IN A NUTSHELL

RAT
CLEVER,
CHARMING,
CURIOUS

OX
PERSISTENT,
STRAIGHTFORWARD,
SINGLE MINDED

TIGER
BRAVE,
INDEPENDENT,
ARROGANT

RABBIT
SENSITIVE, SINCERE,
CAUTIOUS

DRAGON
STRONG, ENERGETIC,
IMPATIENT

SNAKE
WISE, CALM,
SUSPICIOUS

HORSE
WARM-HEARTED,
INDEPENDENT,
LAID BACK

GOAT
CREATIVE,
DEPENDABLE,
CALM

MONKEY
SMART,
ENTERTAINING,
NAUGHTY

ROOSTER
INDUSTRIOUS,
HONEST, AMBITIOUS

DOG
LOYAL, ENERGETIC,
COURAGEOUS

PIG
WELL-MANNERED,
GOOD-TEMPERED, KIND

WHO ARE YOU?

Track down your animal by finding
your birthday in these handy charts

1936 – 1948

24 JAN 1936 – 10 FEB 1937	RAT
11 FEB 1937 – 30 JAN 1938	OX
31 JAN 1938 – 18 FEB 1939	TIGER
19 FEB 1939 – 7 FEB 1940	RABBIT
8 FEB 1940 – 26 JAN 1941	DRAGON
27 JAN 1941 – 14 FEB 1942	SNAKE
15 FEB 1942 – 4 FEB 1943	HORSE
5 FEB 1943 – 24 JAN 1944	GOAT
25 JAN 1944 – 12 FEB 1945	MONKEY
13 FEB 1945 – 1 FEB 1946	ROOSTER
2 FEB 1946 – 21 JAN 1947	DOG
22 JAN 1947 – 9 FEB 1948	PIG

1948 – 1960

10 FEB 1948 – 28 JAN 1949	RAT
29 JAN 1949 – 16 FEB 1950	OX
17 FEB 1950 – 5 FEB 1951	TIGER
6 FEB 1951 – 26 JAN 1952	RABBIT
27 JAN 1952 – 13 FEB 1953	DRAGON
14 FEB 1953 – 2 FEB 1954	SNAKE
3 FEB 1954 – 23 JAN 1955	HORSE
24 JAN 1955 – 11 FEB 1956	GOAT
12 FEB 1956 – 30 JAN 1957	MONKEY
31 JAN 1957 – 17 FEB 1958	ROOSTER
18 FEB 1958 – 7 FEB 1959	DOG
8 FEB 1959 – 27 JAN 1960	PIG

1960 – 1972

28 JAN 1960 – 14 FEB 1961	RAT
15 FEB 1961 – 4 FEB 1962	OX
5 FEB 1962 – 24 JAN 1963	TIGER
25 JAN 1963 – 12 FEB 1964	RABBIT
13 FEB 1964 – 1 FEB 1965	DRAGON
2 FEB 1965 – 20 JAN 1966	SNAKE
21 JAN 1966 – 8 FEB 1967	HORSE
9 FEB 1967 – 29 JAN 1968	GOAT
30 JAN 1968 – 16 FEB 1969	MONKEY
17 FEB 1969 – 5 FEB 1970	ROOSTER
6 FEB 1970 – 26 JAN 1971	DOG
27 JAN 1971 – 14 FEB 1972	PIG

1972 – 1984

15 FEB 1972 – 2 FEB 1973	RAT
3 FEB 1973 – 22 JAN 1974	OX
23 JAN 1974 – 10 FEB 1975	TIGER
11 FEB 1975 – 30 JAN 1976	RABBIT
31 JAN 1976 – 17 FEB 1977	DRAGON
18 FEB 1977 – 6 FEB 1978	SNAKE
7 FEB 1978 – 27 JAN 1979	HORSE
28 JAN 1979 – 15 FEB 1980	GOAT
16 FEB 1980 – 4 FEB 1981	MONKEY
5 FEB 1981 – 24 JAN 1982	ROOSTER
25 JAN 1982 – 12 FEB 1983	DOG
13 FEB 1983 – 1 FEB 1984	PIG

1984 - 1996

2 FEB 1984 - 19 FEB 1985	RAT
20 FEB 1985 - 8 FEB 1986	OX
9 FEB 1986 - 28 JAN 1987	TIGER
29 JAN 1987 - 16 FEB 1988	RABBIT
17 FEB 1988 - 5 FEB 1989	DRAGON
6 FEB 1989 - 26 JAN 1990	SNAKE
27 JAN 1990 - 14 FEB 1991	HORSE
15 FEB 1991 - 3 FEB 1992	GOAT
4 FEB 1992 - 22 JAN 1993	MONKEY
23 JAN 1993 - 9 FEB 1994	ROOSTER
10 FEB 1994 - 30 JAN 1995	DOG
31 JAN 1995 - 18 FEB 1996	PIG

1996 - 2008

19 FEB 1996 - 6 FEB 1997	RAT
7 FEB 1997 - 27 JAN 1998	OX
28 JAN 1998 - 15 FEB 1999	TIGER
16 FEB 1999 - 4 FEB 2000	RABBIT
5 FEB 2000 - 23 JAN 2001	DRAGON
24 JAN 2001 - 11 FEB 2002	SNAKE
12 FEB 2002 - 31 JAN 2003	HORSE
1 FEB 2003 - 21 JAN 2004	GOAT
22 JAN 2004 - 8 FEB 2005	MONKEY
9 FEB 2005 - 28 JAN 2006	ROOSTER
29 JAN 2006 - 17 FEB 2007	DOG
18 FEB 2007 - 6 FEB 2008	PIG

2008 - 2020

7 FEB 2008 - 25 JAN 2009	RAT
26 JAN 2009 - 13 FEB 2010	OX
14 FEB 2010 - 2 FEB 2011	TIGER
3 FEB 2011 - 22 JAN 2012	RABBIT
23 JAN 2012 - 9 FEB 2013	DRAGON
10 FEB 2013 - 30 JAN 2014	SNAKE
31 JAN 2014 - 18 FEB 2015	HORSE
19 FEB 2015 - 7 FEB 2016	GOAT
8 FEB 2016 - 27 JAN 2017	MONKEY
28 JAN 2017 - 15 FEB 2018	ROOSTER
16 FEB 2018 - 4 FEB 2019	DOG
5 FEB 2019 - 24 JAN 2020	PIG

2020 - 2032

25 JAN 2020 - 11 FEB 2021	RAT
12 FEB 2021 - 31 JAN 2022	OX
1 FEB 2022 - 21 JAN 2023	TIGER
22 JAN 2023 - 9 FEB 2024	RABBIT
10 FEB 2024 - 28 JAN 2025	DRAGON
29 JAN 2025 - 16 FEB 2026	SNAKE
17 FEB 2026 - 5 FEB 2027	HORSE
6 FEB 2027 - 25 JAN 2028	GOAT
26 JAN 2028 - 12 FEB 2029	MONKEY
13 FEB 2029 - 2 FEB 2030	ROOSTER
3 FEB 2030 - 22 JAN 2031	DOG
23 JAN 2031 - 10 FEB 2032	PIG

ELEMENT	**WATER**
ENERGY	**YANG**
SEASON	**AUTUMN**
FLOWER	**LILY**
COLOURS	**BLUE**
	GOLD
	GREEN
STONE	**GARNET**
NAMES	**ROLAND**
	REMY
	TEMPLETON
	EMILE
	NIGEL

RAT

24 JANUARY 1936 - 10 FEBRUARY 1937
10 FEBRUARY 1948 - 28 JANUARY 1949
28 JANUARY 1960 - 14 FEBRUARY 1961
15 FEBRUARY 1972 - 2 FEBRUARY 1973
2 FEBRUARY 1984 - 19 FEBRUARY 1985
19 FEBRUARY 1996 - 6 FEBRUARY 1997
7 FEBRUARY 2008 - 25 JANUARY 2009
25 JANUARY 2020 - 11 FEBRUARY 2021

YOUR RAT PERSONALITY

MALE

BORN IN	YOUR TRAITS
1948-49 OR **2008-09** EARTH RAT	**DISCIPLINED**: your gnashers are very clean **LOYAL**: your friends refer to you as 'Dear Ratty' **MATERIALISTIC**: you have too many trainers
1960-61 OR **2020-21** METAL RAT	**EMOTIONAL**: you are prone to making a drama out of buying a bag of fries **MORALISTIC**: you do love a cause **JEALOUS**: your eyes turn green just thinking about the size of your neighbour's new shed
1984-85 WOOD RAT	**ADVENTUROUS**: you are never happier than when wild swimming in the nude **EGOTISTICAL**: you post photos on Instagram of you, wild swimming in the nude **INSPIRATIONAL**: your many followers are prepared to jump in the muddy river after you
1936-37 OR **1996-97** FIRE RAT	**COMPETITIVE**: 'last one up the drainpipe is a mouse' **EXCITING**: you drive lad and lady rats wild **ENERGETIC**: you love nothing more than chasing your tail, round and round
1972-73 WATER RAT	**CLEVER**: you learnt all your times tables before the age of seven **INSTINCTIVE**: you always know when it's time for a nap **TALKATIVE**: chat chat chat and snooze

FEMALE

BORN IN

YOUR TRAITS

1948-49 OR **2008-09**
EARTH RAT

RISK-TAKING: this week you bought 2 lottery tickets
HARD-WORKING: if there's a hole that needs digging you've got your shovel at the ready
INDECISIVE: should you use a shovel or would a fork work better?

1960-61 OR **2020-21**
METAL RAT

HONEST: you're the first to point out a bogey
IDEALISTIC: you have cut palm oil out of your daily life, you're a bit smelly but it's worth it
EMOTIONAL: no one understands how sad adverts are these days

1984-85
WOOD RAT

PEACE-LOVING: you love a good book and a snooze and maybe a back scratch
SOCIABLE: you are happiest when topping up glasses
FLEXIBLE: yogi is your middle name

1936-37 OR **1996-97**
FIRE RAT

WARRIOR-LIKE: you can always sniff out an adversary and they better watch out as you are fiery as well as furry
GENEROUS: in your pocket there is always a clean(ish) handkerchief for those in need
INDEPENDENT: sometimes you tie your own laces

1972-73
WATER RAT

INQUISITIVE: the posh word for nosey
RESPECTFUL: you never kiss on the first date but would break that rule for Tom Holland
INFLUENCER: you change people's lives by posting pictures of what you eat for lunch

WHICH RAT ARE YOU?

So you think you're a rat? But are you wooden or made of steel? This all depends on when you were born...

24 JAN 1936 - 10 FEB 1937 .... **FIRE RAT**
10 FEB 1948 - 28 JAN 1949 .... **EARTH RAT**
28 JAN 1960 - 14 FEB 1961 ....**METAL RAT**
15 FEB 1972 - 2 FEB 1973 .... **WATER RAT**
2 FEB 1984 - 19 FEB 1985.....................**WOOD RAT**
19 FEB 1996 - 6 FEB 1997......................... **FIRE RAT**
7 FEB 2008 - 25 JAN 2009.................. **EARTH RAT**
25 JAN 2020 - 11 FEB 2021...................**METAL RAT**

WOOD RAT...SERENE

Everyone likes you, you are calm, generous and peace-loving, a-twitch with good humour. You work hard to provide a secure home with nice carpets throughout and to have nice long-haul holidays. You are super-competitive but believe success has to be earned and not just grabbed, like some of those other dirty rats might do.

FIRE RAT...BIT FISTY

You are the Indiana Jones of the rat world, with a lust for life and an unquenchable thirst for adventure. Your warrior-like spirit is always looking for a cause to fight, you are definitely more of a fighter than a lover. That said, you are the most generous of all of the rats, regularly donating to the food bank and giving up your seat for pregnant ladies (fingers crossed they're not just fat). Not one to be tied down, you are intrepid in your search for the best curry house in town, always your takeaway of choice.

EARTH RAT...SORTED

You like everything in your life to be orderly; a great day is one spent trying to locate the bottom of the laundry basket. You set yourself realistic goals and buy everyone a Christmas present by the end of November...and what a gift-giver you are, always generous and thoughtful. Be careful not to be too focused on what others think, two Instagram likes are better than none. Your love of all things sweet can lead to big dentist bills.

METAL RAT...THE RUTHLESS

You are no coachman, you are Prince or Princess Charming, the most delightful of all the rats and very sociable too, but underneath that charm you are as hard as nails. Ruthless when it comes to getting what you want, you are like a hot cross rat and outspoken to those who don't meet your exacting standards (they probably had it coming). You keep a lovely home, straight from the pages of a glossy magazine and have a strict 'shoes off at the door' policy. That said, you are the first to welcome in your family and friends.

WATER RAT...BIT OF A WUSS

As a Water Ratty you prefer to go with the flow down stream than swim against the tide, you are always calm in the face of adversity but can be a scaredy rat at times.

You more than make up for this by being kind and you care deeply about tradition...though 'Bash the Rat' isn't one of your favourites...you have a deep-set fear of the summer fête season. That doesn't mean that you are unsociable, far from it you love being with people.

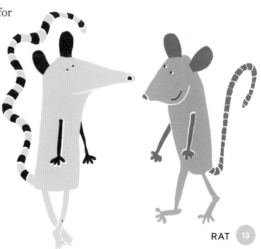

RAT IN LOVE

Are you a rat? Are you sure about that? Is it worth just double-checking your birthday against the chart?

YES   NO → → → →

MALE RAT
↓
YOU ARE

TENDER (when cooked for 2 minutes each side). **THOUGHTFUL** with tailor-made playlists **HONEST** like a good boy scout you always do your best and wear a clean vest.

↓

YOU SHOULD
↓

 **SNAKE**

You are both uplifting and fun but make sure snake has already had her tea.

 **OX**

A faithful and intimate life together bearing lots of baby ratoxen.

 **HORSE**

Too much time taking selfies, not enough time loving each other.

→ → → → You are reading
the wrong chapter

FEMALE RAT
↓
YOU ARE

NAIVE you think you are the only one. **SWEET** you offer to pay the bill. **ROMANTIC** always ready to whisper sweet nothings, with a mouthful of sweets.

↓

YOU DON'T NEED A PARTNER
BUT IF YOU HAVE TO, YOU SHOULD

↓

SNOG ➡ **DRAGON**   If fiery kisses are your thing.

MARRY ➡ **DOG**   A match based on mutual respect, but you could both become quite boring.

AVOID ➡ **ROOSTER**   A bit pecky and not overly affectionate.

RAT AT WORK AND PLAY

RAT WORK

You are clever and hard-working, although quite small you're very good at looking at the big picture. You bring creativity to problem solving, often nipping problems in the bum before they arise. You should aim to be the boss... as Big Boss Rat you will be respected by all worker rats for your wisdom and ability to turn water into wine and then into hard cash. You are not so good at all the HR stuff and also pretty rubbish at sales.

YOUR BEST JOBS

Survivalist

Fashion designer

Racing driver

Caricature artist

Oil worker

Stand-up comedian

YOUR BEST BUSINESS PARTNER

DRAGON   Always knows how to close the sale despite the hot air.

OX   You make all the decisions and just tell ox what to do.

PIG   The potential to make big bucks together.

PASTIMES AND HOBBIES

Selling stuff on Ebay
(to make money)

Learning a foreign language
(to make money)

Eating chocolate (for energy
to make more money)

Making ceramic pots (to sell
at a Sunday market)

HEALTH AND LIFESTYLE

You are pretty healthy as you are always on the go, all the to-ing and fro-ing
can leave you out of breath, so watch out for respiratory problems. Make
sure you wear a nice woolly jumper in cold weather. You can be prone to skin
problems, so make sure you have a good cleansing routine in place to keep
pimples at bay and drink more water than wine.

CELEBRITY RATS

MARK ZUCKERBERG
14 May 1984

Super sociable rat, likes
connecting people.

KATY PERRY
25 October 1984

Partial to German
piped music and has
millions of followers.

ROSA PARKS
4 February 1913

Ratactivist who rightly
refused to give up her
bus seat.

WILLIAM SHAKESPEARE
26 April 1564

Should have called it
'The Taming of the Rat'.

PRINCE HARRY
15 September 1984

A not so royal rat with
an American twang.

SCARLET JOHANSSON
22 November 1984

Adored by rat fans for
her fine gnashers. Likes
a bit of cheese porn.

ELEMENT	**EARTH**
ENERGY	**YIN**
SEASON	**WINTER**
FLOWERS	**TULIP**
	BLOSSOM
COLOURS	**RED**
	BLUE
	PURPLE
STONES	**AQUAMARINE**
	JADE
	AGATE
NAMES	**BULLY**
	FERDINAND
	OTIS
	ELSIE
	CLARABELLE

OX

- - - - - - - - - - - - - - - -

11 FEBRUARY 1937 - 30 JANUARY 1938
29 JANUARY 1949 - 16 FEBRUARY 1950
15 FEBRUARY 1961 - 4 FEBRUARY 1962
3 FEBRUARY 1973 - 22 JANUARY 1974
20 FEBRUARY 1985 - 8 FEBRUARY 1986
7 FEBRUARY 1997 - 27 JANUARY 1998
26 JANUARY 2009 - 13 FEBRUARY 2010
12 FEBRUARY 2021 - 31 JANUARY 2022

YOUR OX PERSONALITY

MALE

BORN IN	YOUR TRAITS
1949-50 OR **2009-10** EARTH OX	**MOTIVATED:** especially by marshmallows **METHODICAL:** you are known for making lists **RELIABLE:** you always bring home the bacon chips
1961-62 OR **2021-22** METAL OX	**QUICK-TEMPERED:** you are always the one who kicks the bucket over **SELF-SUFFICIENT:** your homebrew is legendary **GENEROUS:** everyone gets the same bonus
1985-86 WOOD OX	**SINCERE:** you are the real deal **AMBITIOUS:** apparently the royal family have a few vacancies **PROBLEM SOLVER:** you can handle just about anything, with the exception of algebra
1937-38 OR **1997-98** FIRE OX	**ASSERTIVE:** you shout out answers to quiz questions on the television **FOCUSED:** as long as you have your air pods in and no one speaks to you **JEALOUS:** you saw her first
1973-74 WATER OX	**POLITE:** you always give up your seat for someone who needs it more, especially if you are sitting next to a smelly person **UNFLAPPABLE:** you tolerate the sound of Aunty Mary munching biscuits with her mouth open **FAR-SIGHTED:** especially now you have your new varifocals

FEMALE

BORN IN	YOUR TRAITS
1949-50 OR **2009-10** EARTH OX	**SMART:** you won 'Guess the number of sweets in a jar' once **INDUSTRIOUS:** you are habitually active; even when asleep you dream about cleaning the kitchen **DIGNIFIED:** you are more like a swan than an ox
1961-62 OR **2021-22** METAL OX	**LIBERAL:** often found sitting on your garden fence **COURAGEOUS:** you tell people when they are singing out of tune **OPEN:** your neighbour hides when he sees you coming
1985-86 WOOD OX	**DOWN-TO-EARTH:** you love rolling around in mud **ELEGANT:** your hairy bits are always neatly trimmed **PASSIONATE:** every night is date night
1937-38 OR **1997-98** FIRE OX	**EMOTIONAL:** you actively avoid rom coms and hospital dramas **FAITHFUL:** you always buy the same brand of washing-up liquid **STRICT:** your Christmas chocolates last you all year
1973-74 WATER OX	**DEVOTED:** you kiss your Ed Sheeran poster goodnight every night **SELFLESS:** you always let someone with only one item in their basket go in front of you at the till **RESPECTED:** people keep giving you apples

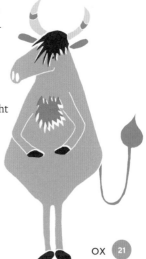

OX 21

WHICH OX ARE YOU?

It might be apparent to all that you're an ox, but I bet you don't know which type of ox you are. Check below please.

11 FEB 1937 – 30 JAN 1938	**FIRE OX**
29 JAN 1949 – 16 FEB 1950	**EARTH OX**
15 FEB 1961 – 4 FEB 1962	**METAL OX**
3 FEB 1973 – 22 JAN 1974	**WATER OX**
20 FEB 1985 – 8 FEB 1986	**WOOD OX**
7 FEB 1997 – 27 JAN 1998	**FIRE OX**
26 JAN 2009 – 13 FEB 2010	**EARTH OX**
12 FEB 2021 – 31 JAN 2022	**METAL OX**

WOOD OX...HARD

You're a leader, you're a leader! You are smart and responsible with a sense of duty to King and country. Not one to show your emotions, if something upsets you then you will cry on the inside like a grown up...though if pushed too hard you can fly into a rage and have been known to kick over the odd potted plant.

FIRE OX...HEADSTRONG

You were not born yesterday and you do not suffer fools. If needed, you will go headlong into battle for what you think is right and any barriers will just be drop-kicked out of the way. You are quite materialistic and count all your money on Mondays. You don't like many people but are quite fond of your family, when they are on their best behaviour.

EARTH OX...THRIFTY

You are a responsible person. Why waste money on designer labels when you can look pretty cool and stay warm in a secondhand cashmere from your local charity shop? You are also kind and fair; you always make sure that everyone gets the same number of peas on their plate. Your attention to detail is second to none and your slow and steady attitude may well win you the race.

METAL OX...READY TO RUMBLE

You are so active and busy that you often forget to eat and sleep...it's just rave repeat for you! You are better at spending than saving...you live for the day. Old age and rainy days can wait. You love a party and make the best Mojito in town, but be careful not to drink too many as you are known for dishing out home truths.

WATER OX...HANDY

You are Peter/Petra Practical, you can turn your hand to most things, but won't waste your time on trifles. You can be a bit of a grump but still gain the respect of those who really know you for your kind heart and ability to fart on demand. All you really want from life is a comfy armchair and the respect of your family and friends.

OX IN LOVE

Are you an ox? Hmm? Well?

YES   NO → → → → ─

MALE OX

↓

YOU ARE

TENDER just like a nice piece of aged steak.
POSSESSIVE you are a bit needy and want
full attention at all times. **ATTENTIVE**
to your partner and many
others at the same time.

↓

YOU SHOULD

↓

SNOG ➡ **ROOSTER**

You two are great together as
long as the rooster doesn't get
in a flap.

MARRY ➡ **RAT**

An unbreakable bond resulting
in lots of babies.

AVOID ➡ **HORSE**

You are a home bird whilst horse
wants to hit the open road.

→ → → You are looking for love in the wrong place, try elsewhere.

FEMALE OX

↓

YOU ARE

DEVOTED you insist on singing songs from Grease to your partner at bedtime. **LOYAL** constantly at your loved one's side, which is a bit annoying when they need to go to the toilet. **JEALOUS** you will pour your rum and coke over the head of anyone who so much as looks at your lover.

↓

YOU SHOULD

↓

SNOG ➡ **OX**
You're happy locking horns with another ox.

MARRY ➡ **SNAKE**
A sweet meeting of minds, both practical and wily.

AVOID ➡ **TIGER**
The only thing you have in common is your stubbornness and a love of dry-roasted nuts.

OX AT WORK AND PLAY

OX WORK

You are great to work with – honest, very hard-working and good with your hands. You complete practical tasks like changing a light bulb or the toilet roll with relative ease and little fuss. You are the most likely of all the signs to see a job through to the end before stopping for a snack. As long as no one interferes with your routine of having a cup of tea and a biscuit at 3 p.m., you are generally an amiable character and well-liked in the workplace. You tend to be a bit secretive about how much you are being paid and about what you do at the weekend.

YOUR BEST JOBS

Dry stone waller

Tax officer

Nail technician

Relationship counsellor

Librarian

Direct marketing assistant

Farmer

Brigadier

YOUR BEST BUSINESS PARTNER

RAT   A good mix of brawn and brain will bring success.

HORSE   Great for manual work, a diligent and caring team that makes for a great finish when plastering.

TIGER   If you both stop complimenting each other and get on with the job, you'll do well.

PASTIMES AND HOBBIES

Watching documentaries

Digging holes in the garden

Board games of all descriptions

Tickling the kids

Cooking in bulk for the week ahead

HEALTH AND LIFESTYLE

You have a strong constitution and are generally healthy with the potential for a long life. You are always working and need to learn how to relax, otherwise you can get stressed and depressed and end up on the sofa watching shopping channels. In your spare time, you generously post ploughing tips online.

CELEBRITY OXEN

BARACK OBAMA
4 August 1961

44th president of USA, pro women for all the right reasons, unlike the 45th.

CHARLIE CHAPLIN
16 April 1889

No need for words, just funny.

MARGARET THATCHER
13 October 1925

Iron lady ox, not one for turning unless tapped on the shoulder.

MALALA
12 July 1997

Nobel and peaceful, needs no other name.

WALT DISNEY
5 December 1901

Always animated, loves a theme park.

GEORGE CLOONEY
6 May 1961

Looks good in scrubs, great in an emergency.

ELEMENT	**EARTH**
ENERGY	**YANG**
SEASON	**SPRING**
FLOWERS	**PLUM BLOSSOM**
	YELLOW LILY
COLOURS	**BLUE**
	ORANGE
	GREY
STONES	**TOPAZ**
	DIAMOND
	AMETHYST
NAMES	**SHERE**
	TIGGER
	TONY
	RICHARD
	SHINE

TIGER

----

31 JANUARY 1938 – 18 FEBRUARY 1939
17 FEBRUARY 1950 – 5 FEBRUARY 1951
5 FEBRUARY 1962 – 24 JANUARY 1963
23 JANUARY 1974 – 10 FEBRUARY 1975
9 FEBRUARY 1986 – 28 JANUARY 1987
28 JANUARY 1998 – 15 FEBRUARY 1999
14 FEBRUARY 2010 – 2 FEBRUARY 2011
1 FEBRUARY 2022 – 21 JANUARY 2023

YOUR TIGER PERSONALITY

MALE

BORN IN	YOUR TRAITS
1938–39 OR **1998–99** **EARTH TIGER**	**AMBITIOUS:** you strive to get into the higher tax bracket **GENEROUS:** you are always the first to get a round in during happy hour **ADVENTUROUS:** you go to Hot Yoga on Mondays
1950–51 OR **2010–11** **METAL TIGER**	**CONFIDENT:** you tell it as it is, but only by email **POWERFUL:** you can cut through grease with your steely glare **STUBBORN:** you will get that marshmallow in that moneybox
1974–75 **WOOD TIGER**	**SENSIBLE:** you always carry your store loyalty cards **EASY-GOING:** your favourite T-shirt is your 'Easy Tiger' **INTELLIGENT:** you have a high IQ, but struggle to remember names
1986–87 **FIRE TIGER**	**AGGRESSIVE:** you prefer 'forceful' and, if others don't agree, you will punch them on the nose **SERIOUS:** you don't get the joke, even when explained **CONSIDERATE:** you sanitize your paws before using the cash machine
1962–63 OR **2022–23** **WATER TIGER**	**SEDATE:** you never run for a bus **CURIOUS:** you always give presents a good feel, even when they're not for you **EGOTISTICAL:** 90% of your phone pics are of you

FEMALE

BORN IN	YOUR TRAITS
1938-39 OR **1998-99** **EARTH TIGER**	**CAREFUL:** you always look three times before crossing **SOCIABLE:** you go to funerals of people you don't know **SUPPORTIVE:** you go to sports day, even though your kids left years ago
1950-51 OR **2010-11** **METAL TIGER**	**VAIN:** you think you are the best thing since sliced bread **SUCCESSFUL:** you won the largest marrow on the allotment competition three years in a row **CHARMING:** the birds come out of the trees for you
1974-75 **WOOD TIGER**	**BRIGHT:** you wear pink trousers with a red jumper **FUN LOVING:** you love flicking people in the head **CAREFREE:** you live for the day, pay day
1986-87 **FIRE TIGER**	**VIGOROUS:** especially when scrubbing pans after a roast **OPTIMISTIC:** your glass is more than half full...of gin and tonic **STRONG:** anyone who defies you will be spun around and tossed over your head
1962-63 OR **2022-23** **WATER TIGER**	**LOGICAL:** you put the heavy things in your shopping bag first, then get someone else to carry it **FRAGILE:** you always give a release pat when hugging, just in case one of your body parts snap **TALENTED:** you can fart the national anthem

WHICH TIGER ARE YOU?

Tiger Tiger, is water, wood, metal, fire or earth your thing? That depends on when you graced the earth with your presence.

31 JAN 1938 - 18 FEB 1939	**EARTH TIGER**
17 FEB 1950 - 5 FEB 1951	**METAL TIGER**
5 FEB 1962 - 24 JAN 1963	**WATER TIGER**
23 JAN 1974 - 10 FEB 1975	**WOOD TIGER**
9 FEB 1986 - 28 JAN 1987	**FIRE TIGER**
28 JAN 1998 - 15 FEB 1999	**EARTH TIGER**
14 FEB 2010 - 2 FEB 2011	**METAL TIGER**
1 FEB 2022 - 21 JAN 2023	**WATER TIGER**

WOOD TIGER...A LAUGH A MINUTE

Of all the tigers you will be the one who has the most 'likes', you are friendly and good-natured, if a little needy. You always acknowledge others when on your morning constitution, but they need to watch out as the next minute you are likely to pounce out on them from behind a tree, always the joker. You are Tigger-like with your bouncy lust for life, but are also easily distracted and want instant results, so a thousand piece jigsaw is not for you.

FIRE TIGER...THE FIRST ON THE DANCE FLOOR

You are eccentric and intelligent, a natural born leader...the one most likely to take charge of the kitty on a pub crawl. You are a great conversationalist, so are always on the guest list for functions and often the centre of attention. Be careful not to let this go to your head as, whilst you're good at getting yourself out of tight spots, a big head can be problematic, especially when buying a hat.

EARTH TIGER...EASILY BORED

You are the ultimate high achiever, always the teacher's pet. Your active mind and tender heart are a winning combination, but you can become restless and often don't do your share of household chores. You think you are clever, but everyone knows that you hide in the toilet (you are just too important to deal with such mundane stuff).

METAL TIGER...LIVING THE HIGH LIFE

Ultimate power is your main focus in all aspects of your life and your willpower is legendary – they won't catch you with your paw in the biscuit barrel. You have your sights set much further and will fight for your right to party. Your cup is most definitely full, in fact it brims over with positivity and Champagne, as you have a taste for the finer things in life.

WATER TIGER...FIRST OFF THE BLOCKS

You were the first of all your friends to pass your driving test. Cautious, calm and a quick learner, you are destined to be behind the wheel. You never complain but you also don't compromise. Your good judgment, work ethic, energy and nice socks mean that you are always picked first for the hockey team.

TIGER IN LOVE

Are you a tiger? Yes, no, don't know? Check the box!

YES

NO → → → → →

MALE TIGER

↓

YOU ARE

LOYAL you follow loved ones around. **POSSESSIVE** you have a vice-like hug, but are very furry. **PASSIONATE** but be careful of sharp nails.

↓

YOU SHOULD

↓

 **SNOG** → **GOAT** Two friends with benefits.

 **MARRY** → **PIG** You always put each other first, even with the bath water.

 **AVOID** → **SNAKE** Snake is too wriggly and has an annoying hiss.

→ → → Wrong time, wrong place, better luck next time.

FEMALE TIGER
↓
YOU ARE

EXCITING often found swinging from the chandeliers. **ROMANTIC** you take pride in squirting ketchup into love hearts. **INDEPENDENT** you like to do the food shop by yourself.

↓

YOU SHOULD

↓

 **SNOG** → **RAT**   You two are made in kissing heaven.

 **MARRY** → **DOG**   And go to couple heaven for ever after, amen.

 **AVOID** → **MONKEY**   You both like the Hazelnut Whirls...it will never work.

TIGER AT WORK AND PLAY

TIGER WORK

You are a born leader. However, if you flunk the interview, consider being a middle manager in the Civil Service – they have flexi time! You are a one-person rapid-response team at work. If there's a problem you will tackle it and solve it with a roar and a beat of your chest. Your personal mantra is 'strive to be better' and you often are, it's not about the money, money, money, for you. With a love of the outdoors you are a best suited to a job that takes you outside for at least part of the day, you need to top up your Vit D.

YOUR BEST JOBS

Human rights lawyer

Police officer

Tabloid newspaper journalist

Manager of a camping store

Ice cream seller

Flight attendant

YOUR BEST BUSINESS PARTNER

HORSE	Long gallops in the fresh air will lead to good business ideas.
RABBIT	A meeting of minds as long as you don't lose your temper. Otherwise, rabbit will scamper off in a huff.
DRAGON	A competent pairing but a lot of hot air.

PASTIMES AND HOBBIES

Midnight rambler – you hope for chocolate not collectors' cards

Martial Arts – master of the high kick

Running marathons in a funny costume

Learning to fly (a drone)

HEALTH AND LIFESTYLE

You tend to pounce on work and enemies. This can leave you mentally and physically exhausted, but you bounce back quickly. You need to find balance in your life for long-term health. Too much red meat can cause problems with your bowels and you must remember to warm up properly before going jogging.

CELEBRITY TIGERS

QUEEN ELIZABETH II
21 April 1926

Better at ruling minions than controlling her brood.

STEVIE WONDER
13 May 1950

Great at birthday parties.

MARILYN MONROE
1 June 1926

Super hot, but unlucky in love.

HARPER LEE
28 April 1926

Wrote good books, had a cute haircut.

USAIN BOLT
21 August 1986

Runs fast, but not good with segways.

VICTORIA BECKHAM
17 April 1974

Posh not posh, known for being fashionable and pouting.

ELEMENT	**WOOD**
ENERGY	**YIN**
SEASON	**SPRING**
FLOWERS	**LILY**
	SNAPDRAGON
COLOURS	**BLACK**
	PINK
	PURPLE
	BLUE
	RED
STONES	**EMERALD**
	JADE
	PERIDOT
	PINK QUARTZ
NAMES	**ROGER**
	JESSICA
	PETER
	BR'ER
	PAT
	BUGS

RABBIT

- - - - - - - - - - - - - - - - - - - -

19 FEBRUARY 1939 – 7 FEBRUARY 1940
6 FEBRUARY 1951 – 26 JANUARY 1952
25 JANUARY 1963 – 12 FEBRUARY 1964
11 FEBRUARY 1975 – 30 JANUARY 1976
29 JANUARY 1987 – 16 FEBRUARY 1988
16 FEBRUARY 1999 – 4 FEBRUARY 2000
3 FEBRUARY 2011 – 22 JANUARY 2012
22 JANUARY 2023 – 9 FEBRUARY 2024

YOUR RABBIT PERSONALITY

MALE

BORN IN	YOUR TRAITS
1939-40 OR **1999-2000** EARTH BUNNY	**EFFICIENT:** you are known for being a bit of a bumlicker **PERSISTENT:** some think you are a stalker **FORESIGHT:** you are a bit of a 'know all'
1951-52 OR **2011-12** METAL BUNNY	**DETERMINED:** go get'em bunny **PRAGMATIC:** both your paws are on the ground **PROUD:** gloating is your thing
1975-76 WOOD BUNNY	**VIRTUOUS:** you write poetry for fun **CHARMING:** you lean up against trees to chat up bunnies **ACTIVIST:** when not leaning on the tree, you're hugging it
1987-88 FIRE BUNNY	**GENTLE:** you're a big wet bunny **FRIENDLY:** you turn up for coffee unannounced **AMBITIOUS:** you drop little pellets on fellow worker bunnies
1963-64 OR **2023-24** WATER BUNNY	**PEACEFUL:** you give hugs not war **CUNNING:** there's always something up your furry sleeve **INTUITIVE:** you hop away at the first sniff of trouble

FEMALE

BORN IN	YOUR TRAITS
1939-40 OR **1999-2000** EARTH BUNNY	**BALANCED:** you've got all the right bits in all the right places **PASSIVE:** your friends describe you as inert **HARMONIOUS:** you whistle a happy tune in the shower
1951-52 OR **2011-12** METAL BUNNY	**INVENTIVE:** you're trying parsnips tonight **PROFESSIONAL:** you wear a hair net when cooking **SECRETIVE:** you have a late night poker habit
1975-76 WOOD BUNNY	**ENERGETIC:** you love a fizzy drink **BRIGHT:** light shines out of your bunny bum **SENSITIVE:** flowers make you sneeze
1987-88 FIRE BUNNY	**CONFIDENT:** you da cocky bunny **PHYSICAL:** you love a bunny bundle **SUCCESSFUL:** you're always top of the bundle
1963-64 OR **2023-24** WATER BUNNY	**SOCIABLE:** you rub paws with the masses **DREAMY:** you often catch yourself dribbling **SELF-SUFFICIENT:** your apple pies are unbeatable

WHICH RABBIT ARE YOU?

You're a rabbit, you're a rabbit, but what type of rabbit are you? It all depends on what year you were born in, as you will have influences from other elements...

19 FEB 1939 - 7 FEB 1940 .... **EARTH RABBIT**
6 FEB 1951 - 26 JAN 1952 .... **METAL RABBIT**
25 JAN 1963 - 12 FEB 1964 ...... **WATER RABBIT**
11 FEB 1975 - 30 JAN 1976 .... **WOOD RABBIT**
29 JAN 1987 - 16 FEB 1988 .... **FIRE RABBIT**
16 FEB 1999 - 4 FEB 2000 .... **EARTH RABBIT**
3 FEB 2011 - 22 JAN 2012 .... **METAL RABBIT**
22 JAN 2023 - 9 FEB 2024 ...... **WATER RABBIT**

WOOD RABBIT...SUPPORTIVE

You're a relaxed little jumper. Generous, cosy, warm and peace-loving; Hygge is your middle name. You love scrambling around among the trees with your mates getting muddy, or planting carrots at your local community garden project. Though you are a clever bunny and extremely resourceful (you can always pull a rabbit out of a hat when needed), you can also be a stubborn little blighter and have a habit of saying the wrong thing.

FIRE RABBIT...HOT STUFF

Full of passion, you are one hot bunny. Bold and bouncy, you seek adventure beyond the burrow. The best communicator of all the bunnies, you are a good choice for best man/chief bridesmaid, as your emotional speeches are famed throughout the land, despite the bad jokes. You are trustworthy, would never nick anyone else's carrots or partner and you prefer conspiracy to confrontation, so can be ninja-like when it comes to delivering chocolate eggs.

EARTH RABBIT...DIGS DEEP

Otherwise known as the clever clogs bunny, you are quiet and wise...busy lining your own burrow and buying lovely things such as posh paw wash and vintage rugs. The most materialistic of all the rabbits, you are hard-working and very good at balancing the books. You can be a little cynical, but when it comes to good advice, you are the go-to bunny.

METAL RABBIT...HARD AS NAILS

Passionate, decisive and sometimes a bit of a brute, you are the iron man/ woman of the rabbit world...others need not apply or indeed mess with you. No one puts Metal Bunny in the corner, as you will come out fighting. A bit of an enigma, you can often be found working under cover of darkness, with cunning that will earn you much respect from fellow rabbits and ultimately ensure a life of Riley.

WATER RABBIT...EAU DE BUNNY

You are a smelly bunny with an aversion to showering, but you do love shooting other bunnies with your water pistol. Despite this, you are really compassionate and the most likeable of all the bunnies, always there with a helping paw and ready to share a carrot. You have a natural aptitude for drama and can often be found in an audition queue for the next big reality TV show. You tend to dwell on the past, just let go of the fact that Earth Bunny collapsed your burrow way back in 1996 whilst jumping around to hip hop tunes and try not to enter into conflict.

RABBIT IN LOVE

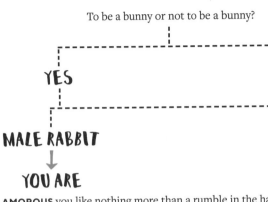

To be a bunny or not to be a bunny?

YES

NO → → →→ -

MALE RABBIT

↓

YOU ARE

AMOROUS you like nothing more than a rumble in the hay.
CAUTIOUS you don't like to be caught in the headlights.
POSSESSIVE you don't share snacks or partners with anyone. If wronged, you have bunny-boiler instincts.

↓

YOU SHOULD

↓

 ➡ **SNAKE**

You are easily seduced by slinky snake, who has oodles of charm.

 ➡ **RABBIT**

You are loved-up bunnies with an appreciation for all the good things. A match that will give you kittens.

 ➡ **TIGER**

Animal print, however much in fashion, is just not you. She is too noisy.

Seek love in another chapter or online.

FEMALE RABBIT

↓

YOU ARE

CALM no fur flying, you're the real Caramel bunny. **KIND** you're always happy to share carrots you have peeled and chopped and made into soup. **FAITHFUL** you're never tempted by greener grass.

↓

YOU SHOULD

↓

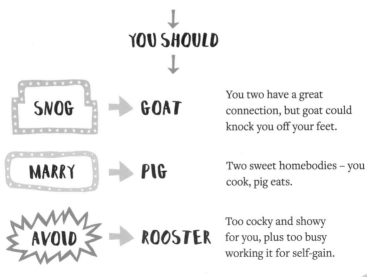

SNOG ➡ **GOAT**
You two have a great connection, but goat could knock you off your feet.

MARRY ➡ **PIG**
Two sweet homebodies – you cook, pig eats.

AVOID ➡ **ROOSTER**
Too cocky and showy for you, plus too busy working it for self-gain.

RABBIT AT WORK AND PLAY

RABBIT WORK

You are great at bringing home the bread (and wilted greens). You are hard-working, successful and good-tempered. You work best with a partner who can give guidance, as when making decisions you can go off-piste, leading to whimsical and non-commercial ideas.
Funny, sweet-natured and positive, you are fun to be around. Everyone likes working with you, especially on a Monday when you bring in a carrot cake you made at the weekend.

YOUR BEST JOBS

Sweet shop owner

MD of a dog-walking business or petting farm

Shakespearean actor

Childrens' party entertainer

Midwife

YOUR BEST BUSINESS PARTNER

HORSE Practical and energetic and good for lifts from A to B.

SHEEP Good at executive decisions and bleating when called for.

DOG Loyal and steadfast, plus happy to clean your wellies.

PASTIMES AND HOBBIES

Gardening, digging, getting muddy and manuring

Spending money on expensive footwear and country attire

Playing the piano whilst sporting an emerald sparkler

Decorating eggs for Easter

Hanging out with friends and family, playing Pass the Pig

High jump or hopscotch

HEALTH AND LIFESTYLE

Whilst physically active and generally healthy, you must watch your diet and not eat too many orange veg or chocolate bars. You can be a bit nervous, try to do 100 bunny hops a day to release endorphins and drink a daily shot of ginger and beetroot juice to help with your digestion and circulation.

CELEBRITY BUNNIES

TIGER WOODS

30 December 1975

The comeback bunny, can always crawl out of the bunker and come out smelling of fresh grass.

MICHELLE OBAMA

17 January 1964

Former first lady Obama bunny is big into chariteeeee and personal appearances.

LIONEL MESSI

24 June 1987

Honest, humble, hard-working bunny, great with balls.

MARGARET ATWOOD

18 November 1939

Quirky, creative-writer bunny who wields a powerful pencil and fights for all female bunnies everywhere.

LIL NAS X

9 April 1999

Loves sequins and a li'l ol' country toon. Coming to a TikTok near you soon.

BRAD PITT

18 December 1963

Handsome L.A. bunny who went down the wrong burrow and ended up with many baby bunnies.

ELEMENT	**EARTH**
ENERGY	**YANG**
SEASON	**SPRING**
FLOWERS	**LARKSPUR**
	BLEEDING HEART
COLOURS	**GOLD**
	SILVER
	GREY
STONES	**AMETHYST**
	SAPPHIRE
	ROSE QUARTZ
NAMES	**ERROL**
	NORBERTA
	RUTH
	ELLIOTT
	PUFF
	DUDLEY
	EDGAR

DRAGON

- - - - - - - - - - - - - - - - - - -

8 FEBRUARY 1940 – 26 JANUARY 1941
27 JANUARY 1952 – 13 FEBRUARY 1953
13 FEBRUARY 1964 – 1 FEBRUARY 1965
31 JANUARY 1976 – 17 FEBRUARY 1977
17 FEBRUARY 1988 – 5 FEBRUARY 1989
5 FEBRUARY 2000 – 23 JANUARY 2001
23 JANUARY 2012 – 9 FEBRUARY 2013
10 FEBRUARY 2024 – 28 JANUARY 2025

YOUR DRAGON PERSONALITY

MALE

BORN IN	YOUR TRAITS
1988-89 **EARTH DRAGON**	**SUCCESSFUL:** you always go down a storm at children's parties **SINCERE:** you make and deliver all your own cards **METICULOUS:** your toe nails are always clean and you are buff
1940-41 OR **2000-01** **METAL DRAGON**	**STRONG-WILLED:** you will huff and you will puff **CLEVER:** you can pat your head and rub your tummy at the same time **BRAVE:** nothing scares you, except public speaking
1964-65 OR **2024-25** **WOOD DRAGON**	**CURIOUS:** you are never happier than when you are twitching a net curtain **IMPULSIVE:** you love a 'buy one get one free' **CREATIVE:** you spend all your cash at craft shops
1976-77 **FIRE DRAGON**	**OUTSPOKEN:** your middle name is often Frank **CHEERFUL:** you whistle as you work **SNEAKY:** you eat two bags of chips but hide the second packet
1952-53 OR **2012-13** **WATER DRAGON**	**PATIENT:** all good things come to you...like Christmas **PRINCIPLED:** you never lick your plate after eating **OPTIMISTIC:** you always live in hope

FEMALE

BORN IN	YOUR TRAITS
1988–89 **EARTH DRAGON**	**PROUD:** you never leave the house in your trackies **SOCIABLE:** you don't just attend book club for the booze **FAIR:** you love all your children equally
1940–41 OR **2000–01** **METAL DRAGON**	**AMBITIOUS:** one day you will own a time share in Alicante **SELF-SUFFICIENT:** you grow your own lettuce **VAIN:** with a butt lift, you would be practically perfect
1964–65 OR **2024–25** **WOOD DRAGON**	**STEADFAST:** you are loyal to soap operas **WELL-MANNERED:** you never tuck in until the gravy is on the table **CONTROLLED:** you only eat the broken biscuits
1976–77 **FIRE DRAGON**	**CONFIDENT:** you are always the best version of yourself **FIERCE:** on Fridays you declare thumb war **STRICT:** you insist that breakages must be paid for
1952–53 OR **2012–13** **WATER DRAGON**	**INTUITIVE:** you knew to buy two bottles of wine **CHEERFUL:** on bad days you turn to ice cream **CALM:** every room in your house has a scented candle

WHICH DRAGON ARE YOU?

Dear Dragon, you might think that you are hot and fiery, but you might be a peace-loving water dragon or a wilful dragon of the wood, it all depends on when you were born...

8 FEB 1940 - 26 JAN 1941 .... **METAL DRAGON**
27 JAN 1952 - 13 FEB 1953 .... **WATER DRAGON**
13 FEB 1964 - 1 FEB 1965 .... **WOOD DRAGON**
31 JAN 1976 - 17 FEB 1977 .... **FIRE DRAGON**
17 FEB 1988 - 5 FEB 1989 .... **EARTH DRAGON**
5 FEB 2000 - 23 JAN 2001 .... **METAL DRAGON**
23 JAN 2012 - 9 FEB 2013 .... **WATER DRAGON**
10 FEB 2024 - 28 JAN 2025 .... **WOOD DRAGON**

WOOD DRAGON...POWER TO THE PEOPLE

You are a true revolutionary who wants to change the world. Motivated, determined and intelligent, you are however not always to be trusted...when it comes to the last Malteser in the box, you tend to think that it has your name on it. You have a sixth sense when it comes to business and your generosity knows no bounds – always willing to share your used tissue or give a sweaty handshake at a moment's notice.

FIRE DRAGON...HUFF AND PUFF

Your energy and initiative will take you a long way, but be careful not to wear yourself out working too hard, eight hours sleep a night will help sort out minor break-outs and baggy eyelids. You are guilty of not always thinking about the consequences of your actions (farting in the office is never acceptable) and watch out for those who want to steal your thunder and your favourite highlighter pens.

EARTH DRAGON...BIG SOFTY

Success is your middle name. You are heading straight to the top of the Christmas tree, the fairy can just move along. You are fierce, but also kind-hearted and always diplomatic about your granny's cheesy quiche. You are unlikely to wear fancy dress as you can't stand anyone laughing at you, but in the bedroom you are a superhero.

METAL DRAGON...HARD WORK

You are the most organized of the dragons – your stationery cupboard is legendary, all your pencils are colour-coded and you love a pack of Post-It notes. Some might consider you a bit obsessive (your love of all things Barbra Streisand) and your sharp tongue has lead to a life of loneliness. That said, you are honest and kind, so if you just learn to keep your trap shut, you might find love one day.

WATER DRAGON...WALLFLOWER

You are a bit of an introvert and like to be private, you have your best ideas in the confines of your own toilet. In fact, there is nothing you find more annoying than having to stand in line for a call of nature. You tend to be a bit of a people pleaser and should think of yourself; it's fine to take the biggest slice sometimes. You are a peaceful dragon and you always have a white hanky in your back pocket to wave in case of emergencies.

DRAGON IN LOVE

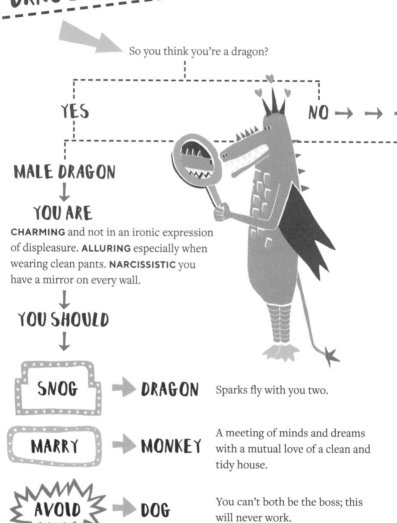

So you think you're a dragon?

YES

NO → → →

MALE DRAGON
↓
YOU ARE

CHARMING and not in an ironic expression of displeasure. **ALLURING** especially when wearing clean pants. **NARCISSISTIC** you have a mirror on every wall.

↓

YOU SHOULD
↓

SNOG ➡ **DRAGON** Sparks fly with you two.

MARRY ➡ **MONKEY** A meeting of minds and dreams with a mutual love of a clean and tidy house.

AVOID ➡ **DOG** You can't both be the boss; this will never work.

You are looking for love in the wrong place, try elsewhere.

FEMALE DRAGON
↓
YOU ARE

ENERGETIC you like all your balls in the air. **DEMANDING** your eggs must be sunny-side-up, semi-soft with soldiers on the side and a blob of ketchup. **SPONTANEOUS** a sudden impulse for a kebab in the middle of the night can lead you anywhere.

↓

YOU SHOULD
↓

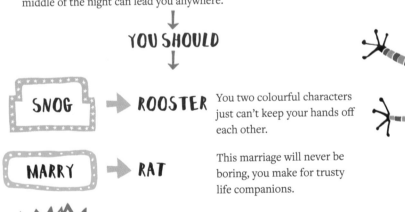

SNOG ➡ **ROOSTER** You two colourful characters just can't keep your hands off each other.

MARRY ➡ **RAT** This marriage will never be boring, you make for trusty life companions.

AVOID ➡ **OX** You are always squabbling and heading in different directions.

DRAGON AT WORK AND PLAY

DRAGON WORK

You can turn your hand to almost anything – plate-spinning, presentations to the board or making a round of tea, you are powerful, hard-working and honest. A dominant character, you make a great leader, mostly (see celebrity dragons). You have a tenacious appetite for business with energy to match – you will always close the deal and are seldom seen without a 1980s briefcase. You are a perfectionist so can be hard to please and tend to favour work over play, unless it's golf.

YOUR BEST JOBS

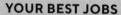

Hardware store owner

Nature photographer

Political commentator

Mixologist

Architect

Fire fighter

YOUR BEST BUSINESS PARTNER

RAT	As long as you are the boss and Rat does as she/he is told.
MONKEY	You are a power couple. Creativity and business acumen will make you loads of money selling funky socks at high prices.
TIGER	You both want to be bad cop, so you're a bit scary.

PASTIMES AND HOBBIES

Burning weeds in the garden – no sweat

Debating society – you love a good argument

Performing magic tricks in front of the mirror

Writing your memoirs at the age of 22

Barbecuing all year round

HEALTH AND LIFESTYLE

You don't have time to get sick because you are too busy working. You are generally very fit and healthy, but can suffer from stress and insomnia. You need to look after your mental health and learn how to relax on a sun-lounger. You must also try to eat more green vegetables with your steak.

CELEBRITY DRAGONS

★ ★ ★

CHARLES DARWIN
12 February 1809

His common ancestor was also a dragon.

ADELE
5 May 1988

Slightly sweary, but knows how to belt out a good tune.

MARTIN LUTHER KING
15 January 1929

A noble, all-round good guy, who died too young.

CHE GUEVARA
14 June 1928

Marxist revolutionary poster boy, looked great in a beret.

VLADIMIR PUTIN
7 October 1952

Powerful, but often forgets to put his top on when going horse riding.

RIHANNA
20 February 1988

Never goes anywhere without her umbrella.

ELEMENT	**EARTH**
ENERGY	**YIN**
SEASON	**SUMMER**
FLOWERS	**ORCHID**
	CACTUS
COLOURS	**RED**
	BLACK
	YELLOW
STONES	**SAPPHIRE**
	AMETHYST
	CARNELIAN
NAMES	**JAKE**
	KAA
	SID
	CY
	KARAI

SNAKE

- - - - - - - - - - - - - - - - - - -

27 JANUARY 1941 – 14 FEBRUARY 1942
14 FEBRUARY 1953 – 2 FEBRUARY 1954
2 FEBRUARY 1965 – 20 JANUARY 1966
18 FEBRUARY 1977 – 6 FEBRUARY 1978
6 FEBRUARY 1989 – 26 JANUARY 1990
24 JANUARY 2001 – 11 FEBRUARY 2002
10 FEBRUARY 2013 – 30 JANUARY 2014
29 JANUARY 2025 – 16 FEBRUARY 2026

YOUR SNAKE PERSONALITY

MALE

BORN IN	YOUR TRAITS
1989-90 **EARTH SNAKE**	**RESERVED:** you dance in the toilet at clubs **KIND:** the exception is when people don't know how to turn right at a box junction, then you are mean **CONTENTED:** you are like a pig in poo
1941-42 OR **2001-02** **METAL SNAKE**	**SECRETIVE:** behind your smile there's a mountain of undisclosed information **FAITHFUL:** you preach about handwashing **COMPETITVE:** you've taken up topiary to outdo your neighbour
1965-66 OR **2025-26** **WOOD SNAKE**	**HARMONIOUS:** but you still haven't learnt how to tune your guitar properly **IDEALISTIC:** you think all will be well if you cough into your elbow **FRIENDLY:** you 'hi-5' kids in pushchairs
1977-78 **FIRE SNAKE**	**DOWN-TO-EARTH:** you keep used tea bags in case you get a sty in your eye **FUNNY:** you make people spray their drinks out of their noses **HARSH:** you always try to beat your kids at chess
1953-54 OR **2013-14** **WATER SNAKE**	**FRUGAL:** you have a small sherry on Sundays **KNOWLEDGABLE:** you impart information to friends and family, but they'd better watch out as you will test them later **SOLITARY:** you can often be found hiding in the shed

FEMALE

BORN IN	YOUR TRAITS
1989-90 **EARTH SNAKE**	**WISE**: you were quick to buy stocks and shares in sanitiser **PATIENT**: it takes a lot to rile you, but people not flushing will do it **GROUNDED**: you cut your own hair
1941-42 OR **2001-02** **METAL SNAKE**	**COOL**: cucumber has got nothing on you **AMBITIOUS**: winning isn't everything, it's the only thing **RUTHLESS**: you have been known to race old ladies to get the last seat on the bus
1965-66 OR **2025-26** **WOOD SNAKE**	**JOYFUL**: your house always smells of freshly baked bread **CLEVER**: you always get the bill to split at restaurants **BOASTFUL**: your Instagram is just you, by the pool, wearing a kaftan, wiggling perfectly polished toes
1977-78 **FIRE SNAKE**	**PRETENTIOUS**: you say that you're writing your memoirs, but you really spend all day in front of the TV **HONEST**: you'd never sell your granny down the river **COURAGEOUS**: you can jump from the top board now
1953-54 OR **2013-14** **WATER SNAKE**	**PROFESSIONAL**: you drive a Lexus **FOCUSED**: you only date one person at a time **MODEST**: you always underestimate the amount of rice to cook

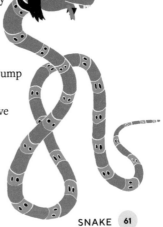

WHICH SNAKE ARE YOU?

When were you born snake? Check below
to see which snake you are.

27 JAN 1941 - 14 FEB 1942 .... **METAL SNAKE**
14 FEB 1953 - 2 FEB 1954 .... **WATER SNAKE**
2 FEB 1965 - 20 JAN 1966 .... **WOOD SNAKE**
18 FEB 1977 - 6 FEB 1978 .... **FIRE SNAKE**
6 FEB 1989 - 26 JAN 1990 .... **EARTH SNAKE**
24 JAN 2001 - 11 FEB 2002.............. **METAL SNAKE**
10 FEB 2013 - 30 JAN 2014............. **WATER SNAKE**
29 JAN 2025 - 16 FEB 2026 .... **WOOD SNAKE**

WOOD SNAKE...STABLE

People are drawn to you like bees are to honey. This is because
you are knowledgeable, honest and witty. You are always willing
to pitch in, whether it's baking cakes for charity, or hosting the
monthly book club. Your love of security and stability does mean
that you have to check that all doors and windows are locked
three times before you leave the house.

FIRE SNAKE...CAN'T SIT STILL

You are a great leader but always make yourself accessible to
your minions, you always leave your office door open, so you
don't miss out on the tea round. You are mentally and physically
active. Even when you are at your computer you rotate your
ankles under your desk, so that you are fit and ready for your
next big adventure.

EARTH SNAKE...CHILL

You are so calm and collected and tune out so much that colleagues once thought you were dead. You lead your life conservatively – just a small scraping of butter on your toast and you never take sugar. You are the one most trusted to cash up and bank the day's takings.

METAL SNAKE...SNEAKY

You are kind and generous, but will still always make sure that you get the biggest scoop and you will only share your crisps if they are cheese and onion flavour. You have incredible willpower so will never over-indulge and you always leave some food on your plate (hidden under your fork, so as not to offend). You are an elusive one and the least likely to divulge your salary.

WATER SNAKE...NOSEY

You are the brightest snake in the den. You don't have many friends but are always invited to the school quiz, as you have an encyclopedic knowledge of just about everything. Your natural curiosity means you have a tendency to curtain-twitch, but only for the greater good of the neighbourhood watch.

SNAKE IN LOVE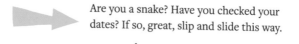

Are you a snake? Have you checked your dates? If so, great, slip and slide this way.

YES

NO → → → → →

MALE SNAKE
↓
YOU ARE

THOUGHTFUL you'll always make breakfast in bed. **FLUSTERED** when in love you are all of a dither. **PASSIONATE** you look deeply into your partner's eyes.

↓

YOU SHOULD
↓

SNOG → **SNAKE**
You know how to press each other's buttons.

MARRY → **MONKEY**
A match made in jungle heaven.

AVOID → **TIGER**
Too much time taking selfies, not enough time loving each other.

Clearly you're not a snake, they would never go to the wrong chapter.

FEMALE SNAKE

↓

YOU ARE

STYLISH onesies are not allowed, silk PJs all the way for you. **INTENSE** your strong feelings and vice-like hugs can take breath away. **WHOLEHEARTED** you are in love with being in love.

↓

YOU SHOULD

↓

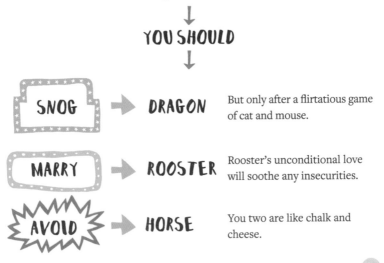

SNOG → **DRAGON**   But only after a flirtatious game of cat and mouse.

MARRY → **ROOSTER**   Rooster's unconditional love will soothe any insecurities.

AVOID → **HORSE**   You two are like chalk and cheese.

SNAKE AT WORK AND PLAY

SNAKE WORK

You need to find a career that will keep you on your toes, where your quick thinking and unique ways will pay dividends. Even though you can't say it, you have a 'sixth sense' for business. You are an enigmatic, tenacious and intelligent leader and a deep thinker. You are great at sealing the deal – you just get them to look into your eyes.

YOUR BEST JOBS

Cruise ship entertainer

Tattooist

Criminal psychologist

Religious minister

Manager of a vintage clothes store

Archaeologist

Bereavement counsellor

YOUR BEST BUSINESS PARTNER

MONKEY   Will push you further up the slippery pole.

ROOSTER   Will calm your nerves with a nice cup of tea.

OX   Very different characters but with similar beliefs – you will bring home the money.

PASTIMES AND HOBBIES

Reading fashion magazines – you like to stay relevant

Going to classical piano concerts

Meditation and mindfulness – you are so of the moment

Going to comedy clubs for open mic night

Polishing your silver until you can see your face in it

HEALTH AND LIFESTYLE

You have it all under control. A good work-life balance will keep you healthy, but try not to over-commit and stretch yourself in all directions, as you will soon burn out.

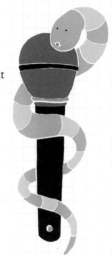

CELEBRITY SNAKES

PABLO PICASSO
25 October 1881

Private man, loved a smoke and swishing a paint brush.

AUDREY HEPBURN
4 May 1929

Gorgeous and had a cat called Cat.

KANYE WEST
8 June 1977

Rich rapper from Atlanta (it rhymes if you speak 'Essex').

J K ROWLING
31 July 1965

Potters about, penning a tale or two.

BUZZ ALDRIN
20 January 1930

First snake in space.

STEPHEN HAWKING
8 January 1942

Only a brief history, but made his mark.

ELEMENT	**EARTH**
ENERGY	**YANG**
SEASON	**SUMMER**
FLOWERS	**JASMIN** **SUNFLOWER** **CALLA LILY**
COLOURS	**RED** **BLUE** **YELLOW** **GREEN**
STONE	**TOPAZ**
NAMES	**RED** **CASS** **DALE** **BESS** **BLAZE** **JOEY** **MERRY** **WINNIE**

HORSE

15 FEBRUARY 1942 - 4 FEBRUARY 1943
3 FEBRUARY 1954 - 23 JANUARY 1955
21 JANUARY 1966 - 8 FEBRUARY 1967
7 FEBRUARY 1978 - 27 JANUARY 1979
27 JANUARY 1990 - 14 FEBRUARY 1991
12 FEBRUARY 2002 - 31 JANUARY 2003
31 JANUARY 2014 - 18 FEBRUARY 2015
17 FEBRUARY 2026 - 5 FEBRUARY 2027

YOUR HORSE PERSONALITY

MALE

BORN IN	YOUR TRAITS
1978-79 **EARTH HORSE**	**PRUDENT:** you only eat red meat on a Sunday and only if someone else has cooked it **IDEOLOGICAL:** you are a Champagne Socialist **HARDWORKING:** You write things on your to-do list after you've done them, just so you can cross them off
1990-91 **METAL HORSE**	**HONEST:** some might say rude **STUBBORN:** you don't clean toilets, never have, never will **INDUSTRIOUS:** you have mastered the art of looking busy
1954-55 OR **2014-15** **WOOD HORSE**	**GOOD-NATURED:** happy to do dressage with kids **SOCIABLE:** the party is always round yours **DEVOTED:** to your job
1966-67 OR **2026-27** **FIRE HORSE**	**PROBLEM-SOLVER:** you love untangling wool **IMPULSIVE:** sometimes you jump on a bus without knowing where it's going **UNPREDICTABLE:** will you wear a blue or a grey suit
1942-43 OR **2002-03** **WATER HORSE**	**LIVELY:** you can't sit still at the table **CHEERFUL:** even in ice cold water **MOODY:** but it doesn't last, as you love slamming doors

FEMALE

BORN IN	YOUR TRAITS
1978 -79 **EARTH HORSE**	**ENERGETIC:** you always use the hill setting on the treadmill **CONTENTED:** especially when you have your wellies on and your binocs round your neck **SENSITIVE:** ice cream always gives you brain freeze
1990-91 **METAL HORSE**	**KIND:** you give your neighbour sugar lumps **PROUD:** your trophies are on display in the hallway **COMMUNICATIVE:** ten words when one would do
1954-55 OR **2014-15** **WOOD HORSE**	**POSITIVE:** you hang out your washing every day in the vain hope that the sun will come out **FRIENDLY:** you love a coffee morning **INSIGHTFUL:** you get itchy armpits when it's about to rain
1966-67 OR **2026-27** **FIRE HORSE**	**IMAGINATIVE:** you tell everyone that you once had tea with all the queen's horses **EMOTIONAL:** You are getting eyeliner tattooed. **BOLD:** you love a red lip, just the top one
1942-43 OR **2002-03** **WATER HORSE**	**WISE:** you can't learn it **EFFICIENT:** you lay out your clothes the night before **IMPATIENT:** It must be five o'clock somewhere

WHICH HORSE ARE YOU?

Dear horse, I know you don't like being told what to do, but you need to check the dates to find out which horse you are.

15 FEB 1942 – 4 FEB 1943.............	**WATER HORSE**
3 FEB 1954 – 23 JAN 1955.............	**WOOD HORSE**
21 JAN 1966 – 8 FEB 1967...................	**FIRE HORSE**
7 FEB 1978 – 27 JAN 1979...............	**EARTH HORSE**
27 JAN 1990 – 14 FEB 1991.............	**METAL HORSE**
12 FEB 2002 – 31 JAN 2003..........	**WATER HORSE**
31 JAN 2014 – 18 FEB 2015.............	**WOOD HORSE**
17 FEB 2026 – 5 FEB 2027.................	**FIRE HORSE**

WOOD HORSE...TECHY

You are the most stable of all the horses; strong as an ox, but with a light heart. You are progressive and imaginative, always with your head in a bit of tech. The only boss of you is you, so heaven help any soul that tells you what to do, as you'll soon kick them into touch, from behind.

FIRE HORSE...SPARKY

You live for the moment, you go skiing at least three times a year, in between city breaks and several trips to Ibiza. Adventure is your middle name, you are always champing at the bit. You are often outspoken but you don't stand still long enough to see whether anyone has taken offence.

EARTH HORSE...THE GOOD LIFE

Everyone has already bolted before you are even off the blocks, but that has never held you back. Your logical brain, quiet resolve and happy disposition make for a good life, the only problem is that you can't decide what socks to wear and that's before you even begin to think about the bigger picture.

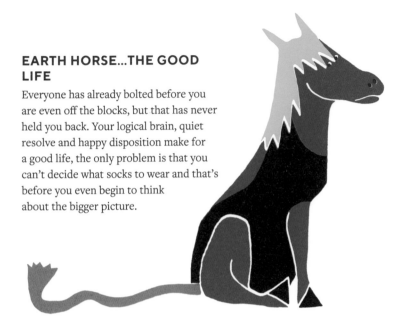

METAL HORSE...NIGHTMARE

You are a 'get things done' type, no trotting about for you, its all 'full throttle' on your production line. You are a bit on the naughty side, a rule breaker with a massive stubborn streak, so anyone that wants to be with you will need to saddle up for the ride. Once you get the bit between your teeth and feel the wind in your hair, you will be off at 90 miles per hour.

WATER HORSE...FLIGHTY

You are the most flexible of the horses (pilates has done you the world of good). You are a real charmer and persuasive too, so make a great sales person. Your restless nature and itchy hooves mean that you are likely to climb to the top quickly, but this does mean that you are often thought to be a bit of a fickle Freddie/Freda.

HORSE IN LOVE

Are you a horsey?
Are you? Are you?

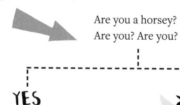

YES

NEIGH → → → →

MALE HORSE

↓

YOU ARE

SHY you still hide behind your mum.
CHARMING all the right words but what about the moves? **DULL** a cup of tea in bed every day gets a bit boring. Mix it up sometimes with a mug of Horlicks.

↓

YOU SHOULD

↓

SNOG → **SNAKE**   You were never going to be just friends.

MARRY → **DOG**   You will live in harmony in a barn conversion.

AVOID → **RABBIT**   Poor rabbit could not keep up with your many needs.

→ → → Look at the contents and try another chapter.

FEMALE HORSE
↓
YOU ARE

REALISTIC you don't expect flowers, so you're never disappointed. **SINCERE** you are genuinely thankful for what you receive. **CONSIDERATE** you eat the dry crust.

↓
YOU SHOULD
↓

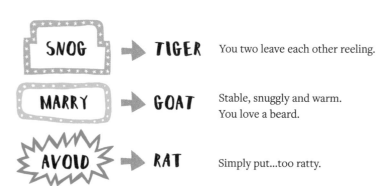

SNOG → **TIGER**   You two leave each other reeling.

MARRY → **GOAT**   Stable, snuggly and warm. You love a beard.

AVOID → **RAT**   Simply put...too ratty.

HORSE AT WORK AND PLAY

HORSE WORK

You need to tame your free spirit in order to do well at work. Bold, active and eloquent you could go the full furlong, with a bit of patience and perseverance. You need a job that will keep you on your hooves and provide change, interest and the chance to get out of the office.

YOUR BEST JOBS

Food critic

Travelling book salesperson

Tour guide

Stockmarket trader

Gallery owner – local crafts

Chilli farmer

Lifelong student

YOUR BEST BUSINESS PARTNERS

TIGER   Fearless when closing the deal.

DOG   You can play bad cop whilst dog gets to run around and lick everyone.

OX   Loyalty and hard work pay off, but ox struggles with your blue-sky thinking.

PASTIMES AND HOBBIES

Cross country running – trot, canter, gallop

Woodland trails – you love bluebells

Making bread and eating it

Carpentry – you are an expert in
making hedgehog houses

Knitting – knit, knit, knitty, knit,
purl one, cast off

Upholstery – you don't like anything that's been stuffed with horse hair

Landscape painting – you are in awe of Constable

HEALTH AND LIFESTYLE

You love green vegetables, the great outdoors and running free. This means that you stay athletic and can live to a ripe old age. Only when caged in a box will you kick out and feel under the weather – it's not good for your mental health. Your love of sugar is your Achille's heel. Try not to crunch sugar lumps as you will end up with big dental bills.

CELEBRITY HORSES

NELSON MANDELA
18 July 1918

27 years in captivity, then took the lead with dignity and grace.

GRETA THUNBERG
3 January 2003

Young environmentalist, teaching world leaders a thing or two.

JIMI HENDRIX
27 November 1942

Favourite colour; purple.

BARBRA STREISAND
24 April 1942

So many gold and platinum albums, they don't fit on the mantelpiece.

ANGELA MERKEL
17 July 1954

Powerful German politician, but a bit shaky if she hasn't eaten her porridge.

JAMES DEAN
8 February 1931

Dead rebel without a cause, looks good in a white unbranded T.

ELEMENT	**EARTH**
ENERGY	**YIN**
SEASON	**SUMMER**
FLOWERS	**CARNATION** **PRIMROSE**
COLOURS	**RED** **GREEN** **PURPLE**
STONE	**EMERALD**
NAMES	**GUSTAV** **DEREK** **GERTRUDE** **BILLY** **NAN** **SHAUN** **BO**

GOAT

- - - - - - - - - - - - - - - - - - - -

5 FEBRUARY 1943 – 24 JANUARY 1944
24 JANUARY 1955 – 11 FEBRUARY 1956
9 FEBRUARY 1967 – 29 JANUARY 1968
28 JANUARY 1979 – 15 FEBRUARY 1980
15 FEBRUARY 1991 – 3 FEBRUARY 1992
1 FEBRUARY 2003 – 21 JANUARY 2004
19 FEBRUARY 2015 – 7 FEBRUARY 2016
6 FEBRUARY 2027 – 25 JANUARY 2028

YOUR GOAT PERSONALITY

MALE

BORN IN	YOUR TRAITS
1979-80 **EARTH GOAT**	**SYMPATHETIC**: you carry plasters in your wallet **FRIENDLY**: your neighbour pretends to be on the phone when he sees you coming **RESPONSIBLE**: you are a primary school governor
1991-92 **METAL GOAT**	**PROUD**: you dress up to go to the supermarket **PURPOSEFUL**: you make sure that your library books are returned on time **GENEROUS**: you buy biscuits you don't like, just to keep everyone else happy
1955-56 OR **2015-16** **WOOD GOAT**	**WARM**: you give free hugs **PERSISTENT**: you are like a dog with a bone **EAGER**: you always volunteer, even when you don't want to
1967-68 OR **2027-28** **FIRE GOAT**	**HEADSTRONG**: another word for pain in the arse **MYSTERIOUS**: are you goat, sheep or wolf in sheep's clothing? **DRIVEN**: you are too busy to play with the kids
1943-44 OR **2003-04** **WATER GOAT**	**BENEVOLENT**: you always put your change in the charity box **POPULAR**: you get likes even when you post pictures of your breakfast **THOUGHTFUL**: you only drink your coffee from a reusable cup

FEMALE

BORN IN	YOUR TRAITS
1979-80 **EARTH GOAT**	**PRACTICAL:** you collect bits of wood; they may have a use one day **FRIVOLOUS:** you shoot passers-by with your water pistol **GIFTED:** you are very good at colouring-in
1991-92 **METAL GOAT**	**ENERGETIC:** you have too many of those green drinks with funny names **CREATIVE:** you make your own soap **PRINCIPLED:** you believe that goats and sheep are equal
1955-56 OR **2015-16** **WOOD GOAT**	**POSITIVE:** there's always someone worse off than you **FIRM:** you have no need for support tights **PEACEFUL:** you like the TV turned down low
1967-68 OR **2027-28** **FIRE GOAT**	**STYLISH:** you'd look good in a plastic bag **SOCIABLE:** you talk to people on public transport **BOLD:** one day you will go into space
1943-44 OR **2003-04** **WATER GOAT**	**PERFECTIONIST:** you never wear lipstick without liner **EMPATHETIC:** you worry when you tread on a snail **GOOD-NATURED:** you don't get cross even when the kid next door kicks his ball into your garden for the fiftieth time

GOAT

WHICH GOAT ARE YOU?

You might have a little manicured beard or you might have clean shaven legs, but do you know which goat you are – wood, fire, earth, metal or water?

5 FEB 1943 – 24 JAN 1944	**WATER GOAT**
24 JAN 1955 – 11 FEB 1956	**WOOD GOAT**
9 FEB 1967 – 29 JAN 1968	**FIRE GOAT**
28 JAN 1979 – 15 FEB 1980	**EARTH GOAT**
15 FEB 1991 – 3 FEB 1992	**METAL GOAT**
1 FEB 2003 – 21 JAN 2004	**WATER GOAT**
19 FEB 2015 – 7 FEB 2016	**WOOD GOAT**
6 FEB 2027 – 25 JAN 2028	**FIRE GOAT**

WOOD GOAT...THE LONER

You like your own company best, but you are always polite and helpful. You can't resist carrying bags for old ladies, even if it does make you late for work. You would make a great Human Rights Lawyer or a Social Worker, but be careful that the baddies don't take advantage of your sweet nature.

FIRE GOAT...TELL US A STORY

Of all the goats you are most likely to stand your ground and not be trampled on. You are easy-going, but courageous. Everyone loves going to the pub with you, as you tell great stories and are the first to get a round in. You are also a loyal friend – their secret will be safe with you. You are well-liked and will do OK for yourself, as long as your expectations aren't too high and you manage your stubborn streak.

EARTH GOAT...CAN NEVER TELL A LIE

You are known for your honesty but sometimes you are a bit too honest. If someone asks you if you like their new hairstyle, it's best not to tell them exactly what you think. Be careful not to hold the door open for too long as people will keep filing through if you let them. Don't go to Bingo – you're not great with money and you are unlikely to win.

METAL GOAT...MADE THE LOCAL NEWS

You are a talented individual, likely to make a splash at the local drama group. You are at your best when you have a routine in place – bed by 10 p.m. and afternoon tea at 3 p.m.. Principled and disciplined, you will be well-respected but some people will find you a bit boring.

WATER GOAT...POOR BUT HAPPY

You are a very appealing goat. Your sensitive nature, creativity and loyalty make you quite a catch, but your tendancy to blow your paycheck the minute you get it, can hold you back. You are more likely to be a poor artist than a multi-millionaire, but (hairy) chin up, you'll always have your mates.

Whether you consider yourself to be goat or sheep trot this way to find your one true love. But first, let's get one thing straight, are you a goat?

YES

NO → → → → →

MALE GOAT

↓

YOU ARE

VAIN you check yourself out in shop windows. **OVER-PROTECTIVE** you always make your partner wear a coat. **CAPRICIOUS** you are known for your roving eye.

↓

YOU SHOULD

↓

SNOG ➡ **MONKEY** Goat and monkey are ever so funky, just made for kissing.

MARRY ➡ **HORSE** You two are perfect hoof mates.

AVOID ➡ **ROOSTER** She's too bossy and might outshine you.

→ → → Bad luck, try another chapter

FEMALE GOAT

↓

YOU ARE

DEVOTED to your cat. **HESITANT** it takes you six weeks to go in for a snog. **SENTIMENTAL** you love a weepy movie and a power ballad.

↓

YOU SHOULD

↓

 **SNOG** → **GOAT**

He's good for a kiss but not much else (too much trotting over the bridge looking for greener grass).

 **MARRY** → **PIG**

You two are the cutest, gentle and cosy...yawn.

 **AVOID** → **DOG**

You are a match made in misery.

GOAT AT WORK AND PLAY

GOAT WORK

You are sure-footed; slowly you will climb the Austrian mountains to achieve good things. You put others before yourself, so will be at your best in a stable environment where you can give back. Your tendancy to eat all the office biscuits will be an annoyance to some, so make sure you make up for it by making plenty of tea.

YOUR BEST JOBS

Postperson

Chiropodist

Life-drawing teacher

Mountain guide

Philosopher

Pole dancer

Beautician

Poet

Marriage counsellor

YOUR BEST BUSINESS PARTNER

HORSE   Many hooves make light work, but you need to work on communication and cut out the naying and braying. A weekly catch up meeting will pay dividends.

SNAKE   You're both happy to share different ideas for a common goal.

RABBIT   Your little creative minds can achieve great things.

PASTIMES AND HOBBIES

Feng Shui – you love anything from Ancient China

Pilates, and stretch

Cake decorating (fancy piping)

Writing a memoir

Decoupage, lick, lick, stick

Interior design and rearranging your cushions

Book club (blah, blah, slurp)

Quilting – you hand stitch so you don't have to rethread your machine

HEALTH AND LIFESTYLE

You are constantly on the look out for your next snack (you are a fridge grazer par excellence). It might be a good idea to try swapping cheese, chocolate and crisps for some really delicious rice cakes or equally scrummy dry breadsticks. In order to live your best life, don't keep slogging up a rugged cliff. Take a chill pill, kick back and relax your little bleating heart.

CELEBRITY GOATS

ED SHEERAN
17 February 1991

Always writing songs that sound the same about girls.

STEVE JOBS
24 February 1955

Apples are not the only fruit.

JULIA ROBERTS
28 October 1967

Pretty actress, smells as good as she looks.

NICOLE KIDMAN
20 June 1967

Actress who likes a bit of country and western.

FRIDA KAHLO
6 July 1907

The original selfie maker, liked an eclectic Mexican outfit.

COCO CHANEL
19 August 1883

Style icon who liked a pearl button.

ELEMENT	**METAL**
ENERGY	**YANG**
SEASON	**AUTUMN**
FLOWERS	**CHRYSANTHEMUM** **ALLIUM**
COLOURS	**WHITE** **BLUE** **GOLD**
STONES	**PERIDOT** **TOPAZ** **RUBY**
NAMES	**ALBERT** **GEORGE** **KOKO** **CLYDE** **VIRGIL** **MARCEL** **FRANCINE** **LOUIE** **ALEX**

MONKEY

- - - - - - - - - - - - - - - - - -

25 JANUARY 1944 – 12 FEBRUARY 1945
12 FEBRUARY 1956 – 30 JANUARY 1957
30 JANUARY 1968 – 16 FEBRUARY 1969
16 FEBRUARY 1980 – 4 FEBRUARY 1981
4 FEBRUARY 1992 – 22 JANUARY 1993
22 JANUARY 2004 – 8 FEBRUARY 2005
8 FEBRUARY 2016 – 27 JANUARY 2017
26 JANUARY 2028 – 12 FEBRUARY 2029

YOUR MONKEY PERSONALITY

MALE

BORN IN	YOUR TRAITS
1968–69 OR **2028–29** EARTH MONKEY	**CAUTIOUS:** your ISA is set to risk level one **COMMUNICATIVE:** you like the sound of your own voice **EMPATHETIC:** you feel the pain of your fellow man when forced to drink bad coffee
1980–81 METAL MONKEY	**SELF-ASSURED:** it's only a matter of time before everyone realizes how amazing you are **MOTIVATED:** it's all about the money for you **OPPORTUNISTIC:** you swing in to steal the last slice of banana cake
1944–45 OR **2004–05** WOOD MONKEY	**CHARMING:** you might seem this way, but you are no prince **VAIN:** you walk around naked with the curtains open **INTUITIVE:** you always know when there's a cake in the oven
1956–57 OR **2016–17** FIRE MONKEY	**DECISIVE:** you'll choose fries every time **IMAGINATIVE:** you cut your toast into heart shapes **TEMPERMENTAL:** you are lovely, lovely, lovely, then mean
1992–93 WATER MONKEY	**CALM:** you take regular rests on the sofa **THOUGHTFUL:** you clean the bath after using it **OBSERVANT:** you know all your neighbours' movements

FEMALE

BORN IN

YOUR TRAITS

1968-69 OR
2028-29
EARTH MONKEY

QUICK-WITTED: you shoot from the hip to amuse yourself
PRAGMATIC: you always make good decisions, usually based on what your tummy is telling you
UNPREDICTABLE: ooh ooh ooh sometimes you're nice, other times you're not

1980-81
METAL MONKEY

FUN-LOVING: you used to hog the swings when you were a kid
POWERFUL: Wonder Woman has got nothing on you
RESOURCEFUL: you make lanterns out of baked bean cans

1944-45 OR
2004-05
WOOD MONKEY

OPTIMISTIC: you feel sure that one day you will get a decent birthday present
PERFECTIONIST: you plan your Christmas table decorations months in advance
ENTERTAINING: you don't need a stage, anywhere will do

1956-57 OR
2016-17
FIRE MONKEY

OUTGOING: you hang around bus stops looking for people to talk to
CALCULATING: you fill the office kettle with just enough water for one cup
CONFIDENT: you have no need for slogan Ts

1992-93
WATER MONKEY

ASTUTE: apart from your secret addiction to the shopping channel
ADVENTUROUS: you wear shorts all year round
POPULAR: in your village

WHICH MONKEY ARE YOU?

You might think you know most things, but do you know which monkey you are? You just need to remember that special day you graced the earth with your presence and check below.

25 JAN 1944 – 12 FEB 1945 .... **WOOD MONKEY**
12 FEB 1956 – 30 JAN 1957 .... **FIRE MONKEY**
30 JAN 1968 – 16 FEB 1969 .... **EARTH MONKEY**
16 FEB 1980 – 4 FEB 1981 .... **METAL MONKEY**
4 FEB 1992 – 22 JAN 1993 ....**WATER MONKEY**
22 JAN 2004 – 8 FEB 2005 .... **WOOD MONKEY**
8 FEB 2016 – 27 JAN 2017 .... **FIRE MONKEY**
26 JAN 2028 – 12 FEB 2029 .... **EARTH MONKEY**

WOOD MONKEY...HEAD IN THE CLOUDS

You are a born optimist, a warm-hearted dreamer, your idea of heaven is gently rocking to and fro in a hammock, in the jungle, with dappled sun on your face and a cocktail in your hand. You work hard to make this dream a reality. Everyone wants you on their team at quiz night, as you have a great memory for useless facts and always turn up on time with loads of snacks.

FIRE MONKEY...YOU THINK YOU'RE FUNNY

You are the cheekiest of all the monkeys; your bare-faced cheeks are often seen outside the pub at kicking-out time. You are eccentric and entertaining, so everyone wants to be your friend, until, lightening-fast, you nick their packed lunch and run off to eat it under a tree. You are restless and driven, you raise the bar, then you raise it further, then you enjoy swinging from it.

EARTH MONKEY...YOU THINK YOU'RE THE POLICE

You are always trying to get to the bottom of things, searching for the truth and for justice. You are principled and law-abiding, although sometimes you have been known to help yourself to a Foam Banana from the pic'n'mix. Ever resourceful and mostly dynamic (though often inert on the sofa on Sunday), you always make time for a friend in need. Your wise counsel and Victoria Sponge are infamous, but they will have to wait until after you have had your morning coffee, or else you will be grumpy.

METAL MONKEY...STOCKPILING FOR THE END OF THE WORLD

You are a closed book and not one to be crossed, else those pages will unleash almighty revenge...don't mess with Metal Monkey! You are also funny and broadminded, with many a trick up your jumper, though you never perform for peanuts. You love making and spending money and have very good taste – it's Champagne and cashmere for a classy monkey like you. Once you have made your mind up about something, there will be no budging you; you are like a monkey mountain.

WATER MONKEY... OF MYSTERY

Oooh you monkey of mystery, you keep it all under your bowler hat. You're a wise monkey that sees and hears, but generally says no evil (still, the kettle's always on for anyone who wants to call in for a brew and a natter). You stand out from the crowd with your love of a tartan trouser and a bow-tie, though heaven help anyone who laughs at you, as they will wound you deeply and risk the wrath of monkey.

MONKEY IN LOVE

Are you a little bit cheeky and do you love bananas? If so, you are probably a monkey, but have you checked your birthday chart?

YES

NO → → → →

MALE MONKEY
↓
YOU ARE

CRAZY buckle up for the ride, you are never boring. **ROMANTIC** you have a rose bush in your garden, ready to pluck at a moment's notice. **GENTLE** you like to groom those you love and pick out their nits and eat them.

↓

YOU SHOULD
↓

 SNOG → **MONKEY** You pair of crazies are good for a one-time-only kiss.

 MARRY → **GOAT** She will keep the finances in check.

 **AVOID** → **TIGER** Ego + ego = no go.

→ → → You got it wrong again...

FEMALE MONKEY

↓

YOU ARE

CARING you have a nurse's outfit in the wardrobe, just in case. **SECRETIVE** what happens on netball tour stays on netball tour. **IMAGINATIVE** you put special ingredients in your cauliflower cheese.

↓

YOU SHOULD

↓

 **SNOG** → **RABBIT** Lovely rabbit is sweet, but not a keeper as too boring.

 **MARRY** → **RAT** You tolerate each other's shortcomings and are mates for life.

 **AVOID** → **PIG** You are both too busy doing your own thang.

MONKEY AT WORK AND PLAY

MONKEY WORK

You need a job where you can work and play at the same time. A 9–5 pen-pushing, desk job is not for you. You like taking calculated risks and can't bear anyone looking over your shoulder or telling you what to do. Your cool head, creative thinking and ability to solve problems mean that it's you that has to sort the coffee machine out when it's broken. You are a bit accident-prone, so it's best that you're not left alone with scissors or scalpels. You make a great leader (you're tickling skills have a way of winning compliance from any doubters).

YOUR BEST JOBS

Venture capitalist

Animal groomer

Cocktail bar owner

Theatre critic

Trapeze artist

Inventor

Tree surgeon

YOUR BEST BUSINESS PARTNER

DRAGON   You two will hit the big time with your fabulous ideas.

RAT   You like working together and love laughing, plus your cunning will bring success.

SNAKE   You are quite similar and, despite mostly being up to mischief, you have similar goals. When you clash, everyone will leave the room.

PASTIMES AND HOBBIES

Tropical plant lover (they don't need much water)

Charity shop browser – you are like a magpie when it comes to finding hidden treasure

Party host (straight from a 70s sitcom)

Blogger (post-breakfast, post-lunch, post-dinner)

Hanging around, people-watching

Snacking, all day long

HEALTH AND LIFESTYLE

You are mainly in robust health and you just get on with it, brushing sore throats and sniffles to one side. Your restless, agitated nature and entrepreneurial lifestyle can mean that hidden anxieties drag you down and make you bite your nails, but a bit of self-care and a good rest will sort you out. Be careful not to get into too many squabbles, if you want to sleep at night.

CELEBRITY MONKEYS

KYLIE MINOGUE
28 May 1968

Sassy little Australian monkey, nice gold shorts.

KIM KARDASHIAN
21 October 1980

Difficult to keep up with this mega-rich, super-glam business woman and mum.

JENNIFER ANISTON
11 February 1969

Always playing the monkey or with a monkey in rom coms and sitcoms.

GEORGE LUCAS
14 May 1944

Responsible for many films with the word 'wars' in the title.

RYAN GOSLING
12 November 1980

An irresistible combination of bird and monkey.

HOMER SIMPSON
12 May 1956

Madcap dad of three, with many hobbies.

ELEMENT	**METAL**
ENERGY	**YIN**
SEASON	**AUTUMN**
FLOWERS	**GLADIOLA**
	IMPATIENS
COLOURS	**GOLD**
	BROWN
	YELLOW
STONE	**CITRINE**
NAMES	**HENNY**
	RED
	CAMILLA
	ROCKY
	ERNIE
	ROY
	BABS
	CLARA

ROOSTER

----

13 FEBRUARY 1945 – 1 FEBRUARY 1946
31 JANUARY 1957 – 17 FEBRUARY 1958
17 FEBRUARY 1969 – 5 FEBRUARY 1970
5 FEBRUARY 1981 – 24 JANUARY 1982
23 JANUARY 1993 – 9 FEBRUARY 1994
9 FEBRUARY 2005 – 28 JANUARY 2006
28 JANUARY 2017 – 15 FEBRUARY 2018
13 FEBRUARY 2029 – 2 FEBRUARY 2030

YOUR ROOSTER PERSONALITY

MALE

BORN IN	YOUR TRAITS
1969–70 OR **2029–30** EARTH ROOSTER	**OBSERVANT:** you take your binoculars with you wherever you go **MISCHIEVOUS:** you give people on escalators wedgies **SHARP:** you laugh when people hurt themselves
1981–82 METAL ROOSTER	**CAPTIVATING:** you are infamous for your boiled egg trick **NEAT:** your T-shirt is always tucked in **IDEALISTIC:** you hope one day to own a caravan
1945–46 OR **2005–06** WOOD ROOSTER	**HONEST:** you would never knowingly tell an untruth **CONGENIAL:** most people consider you to be quite pleasant **OPINIONATED:** you read broad sheets in the toilet
1957–58 OR **2017–18** FIRE ROOSTER	**INDUSTRIOUS:** you always carry over annual leave **INDEPENDENT:** you are self-governing **AUTHORITATIVE:** you are always right
1993–94 WATER ROOSTER	**CULTURED:** you have afternoon tea at 3 p.m. **EFFICIENT:** you file your tax return in April **RESOURCEFUL:** you could live off chocolate if you had to

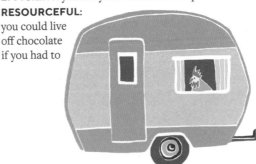

FEMALE

BORN IN

YOUR TRAITS

1969–70 OR
2029–30
EARTH ROOSTER

PERFECTIONIST: you iron your knickers
IMAGINATIVE: you pick up other people's rubbish and make it into small ornaments
ENIGMATIC: you're a mystery, even to yourself

1981–82
METAL ROOSTER

FAITHFUL: you always make the same cake
CARING: in your spare time you play the piano at care homes
PRECISE: every week you sharpen all your pencils

1945–46 OR
2005–06
WOOD ROOSTER

SOCIABLE: you make friends easily, then spend a year trying to shake them off
CHARISMATIC: religious cult leaders have nothing on you
METICULOUS: you are too hung up on small details

1957–58 OR
2017–18
FIRE ROOSTER

FEARLESS: you were born brave but don't care too much for the dark
ELEGANT: you always give one too many kisses
UNCOMPLICATED: you don't have any emotional baggage

1993–94
WATER ROOSTER

GENTLE: people often ask you to speak up a bit
TACTFUL: you brush people off as sensitively as possible
WISE: you sound just like your mum

WHICH ROOSTER ARE YOU?

Hey bird, don't ruffle your feathers, just look yourself up using the list below...you're one of the five.

13 FEB 1945 - 1 FEB 1946	**WOOD ROOSTER**
31 JAN 1957 - 17 FEB 1958	**FIRE ROOSTER**
17 FEB 1969 - 5 FEB 1970	**EARTH ROOSTER**
5 FEB 1981 - 24 JAN 1982	**METAL ROOSTER**
23 JAN 1993 - 9 FEB 1994	**WATER ROOSTER**
9 FEB 2005 - 28 JAN 2006	**WOOD ROOSTER**
28 JAN 2017 - 15 FEB 2018	**FIRE ROOSTER**
13 FEB 2029 - 2 FEB 2030	**EARTH ROOSTER**

WOOD ROOSTER...SANTA'S LITTLE HELPER

You don't need to be the centre of attention like some of the other showy birds, you are simply pleasant and down to earth. You seldom raise your head above the parapet or put up your hand, unless you really need to go to the toilet. Sometimes you can be irresponsible, but underneath all those feathers you are quietly caring and always ready to give a helping hand.

FIRE ROOSTER...LEADER OF THE PACK

You are the leader of the birds; great at planning and able to multi-task (you can talk on the phone whilst tweeting). Your easy-going style will often find you with your feet up on the desk – it's how you have your best ideas. You are known for bad jokes that are only funny because of the way you tell them.

EARTH ROOSTER...UNDERSTATED

Forget the show of feathers, you are no gaudy, strutting bird. Instead, you are quietly engaging, although your sneezes can often be heard on the other side of town. You are honest and inquisitive, but your constant questioning and thirst for knowledge can be quite annoying at times. Though dynamic, you tend to be easily distracted, so can take some time to finish anything and the perfectionist in you means that you should charge by the hour and not for the job.

METAL ROOSTER...WINNER WINNER...

You want to be top of the tree and will trample over others to claw your way up there. You have many minions who will happily stroke your ego on demand. You are best left to your own devices, as you will undoubtedly do the best job, your beady rooster eyes are always focused on the prize. But you're not all bad, you are happy to chuck a coin in a charity box and there is nothing more important to you than family.

WATER ROOSTER...YOU STRUT

You are the smartest of our feathered friends. You look good and are always first off the block (there are no mites on you). You are nice-natured and gentle, but can be a bit of a show-off. Like a child or a magpie, you love collecting shiny things – can-pulls and sea glass – but that said, you can never remember where you put your keys.

ROOSTER IN LOVE

You're a snappy dresser with oodles of charm, but are you really a rooster? Can you cock-a-doodle-doo?

YES ···· **NO** → → → → —

MALE ROOSTER

↓

YOU ARE

PEDANTIC you love giving constructive criticism. **EBULLIENT** whatever your age you are still a chick at heart. **THOUGHTFUL** you give really great gifts, when you remember.

↓

YOU SHOULD

↓

BIRD SEED

SNOG → **SNAKE**
You two are all about seduction and exxxxxcitement.

MARRY → **MONKEY**
You like each other's minds, though it's often love and hate, but love will win out, you are in it for the long run.

AVOID → **ROOSTER**
You two fight from dawn to dusk.

Wrong again,
must try harder...

→ → →

- - - - - - - - - - - - -

FEMALE ROOSTER

↓

YOU ARE

MYSTERIOUS you like to keep them guessing. **AUDACIOUS** you are no wallflower. **OPEN-MINDED** though you draw the line at toes.

↓

YOU SHOULD

↓

SNOG ➡ **HORSE** It's worth your pizza going cold for.

MARRY ➡ **DRAGON** Mutual admiration and wisdom make for a solid life.

AVOID ➡ **TIGER** You have nothing in common; feather and fur, don't go there.

ROOSTER AT WORK AND PLAY

ROOSTER WORK

You're up and crowing at the crack of dawn, another day to busy yourself doing everyone elses' jobs. You are the first in to work and usually your dinner is in the dog by the time you get home. You just don't know how to rest, let alone sit still as you're always pecking away at something. It's not about the money for you, but about making a difference, doing a great job and getting adoration from your many fans. You constantly need to be challenged, but must have your own space to perform, if there's one thing you can't abide it's being cooped up.

YOUR BEST JOBS

Spy

Astronaut

Art historian

Pantomine dame

Comic book illustrator

Cage fighter

Weather person

YOUR BEST BUSINESS PARTNER

DRAGON Dragon is the backbone whilst you are Art Director.

MONKEY You two are a funny old mix that works, the job would be done sooner if you spent less time finding each other so amusing.

DOG A successful pairing, dog is happy for you to be the boss if you scratch his/her back every so often.

PASTIMES AND HOBBIES

Amateur dramatics, darling

Stamp collecting (but not ones that have been licked)

Vintage car rallies – you love an old banger

Rock and gem fairs and heavy rock concerts

Wild swimming (but always in a wet suit)

Quad biking – everyone can eat your dust

Festivals – anything to dodge the soap

Bird watching (you love a feathered friend)

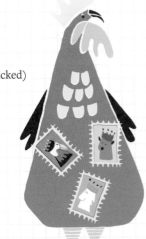

HEALTH AND LIFESTYLE

You are pretty healthy as you're always on the go, but you wouldn't think so to listen to you. Your long list of minor ailments is enough to drive anyone that can be bothered to listen, either to sleep or up the wall. The best way for roosters to stay healthy is to be less fussy about their food and manage their oversensitive personality. Also, an unhealthy desire to stay looking young and stay current is as worthwhile as trying to turn back the tide.

CELEBRITY ROOSTERS

BOB MARLEY
6 February 1945

Had three little birds on his doorstep.

MATTHEW PERRY
19 August 1969

He never remembers friends' birthdays.

HARRY STYLES
1 February 1994

Aptly named, made pearls fashionable again.

SERENA WILLIAMS
26 September 1981

Boy can she hit a ball.

MEGHAN MARKLE
4 August 1981

One time actress, a Sussex, but not a royal.

DOLLY PARTON
19 January 1946

Here she comes again.

ELEMENT	**EARTH**
ENERGY	**YANG**
SEASON	**AUTUMN**
FLOWERS	**ROSE**
	ORCHID
COLOURS	**GREEN**
	RED
	PURPLE
STONE	**DIAMOND**
NAMES	**BOO**
	NELL
	CLIFFORD
	BENJI
	ROLF
	FIFI
	REX
	FLOSS
	DUSTY

DOG

- - - - - - - - - - - - - - - - - - - -

2 FEBRUARY 1946 – 21 JANUARY 1947
18 FEBRUARY 1958 – 7 FEBRUARY 1959
6 FEBRUARY 1970 – 26 JANUARY 1971
25 JANUARY 1982 – 12 FEBRUARY 1983
10 FEBRUARY 1994 – 30 JANUARY 1995
29 JANUARY 2006 – 17 FEBRUARY 2007
16 FEBRUARY 2018 – 4 FEBRUARY 2019
3 FEBRUARY 2030 – 22 JANUARY 2031

YOUR DOG PERSONALITY

MALE

BORN IN	YOUR TRAITS
1958-59 OR **2018-19** EARTH DOG	**LAID BACK:** you need an afternoon nap **RESPECTED:** you have an open door policy at work **PRACTICAL:** you carry a mini tool kit from a Christmas cracker in your back pocket
1970-71 OR **2030-31** METAL DOG	**FAIR:** you apply lemon juice to your hair on holiday **GENEROUS:** you buy extra trick or treat sweets, if they don't all get eaten, you can have some yourself **PRINCIPLED:** in online auctions, you only buy items that charge the correct postage
1994-95 WOOD DOG	**FRIENDLY:** you look forward to catching up with the window cleaner **SUPPORTIVE:** you wear your 'You Got This' T-shirt to sales pitches **SERIOUS:** you like extra strong cheese
1946-47 OR **2006-07** FIRE DOG	**EMOTIONAL:** you love a birthday card with a heartfelt sentiment **AMBITIOUS:** you hope one day to make your own yogurt **RESPONSIBLE:** you wear a visibility vest after 6 p.m.
1982-83 WATER DOG	**INTUITIVE:** you know when it is tea time **PROBLEM SOLVER:** though you still have to work out whether jam or cream comes first on a scone **INDECISIVE:** your underwear have the days of the week printed on, to make life easier

FEMALE

BORN IN	YOUR TRAITS
1958-59 OR **2018-19** **EARTH DOG**	**PEACEFUL:** when you have your headphones on **PATIENT:** you don't mind queuing at supermarkets, as you like looking into other people's baskets **ORGANIZED:** Christmas comes with its own spread sheet
1970-71 OR **2030-31** **METAL DOG**	**STRONG:** you drink beer for breakfast **CONTROLLED:** you take just one muffin from the all-inclusive breakfast buffet **STUBBORN:** you are immovable, like a bad stain
1994-95 **WOOD DOG**	**CHARMING:** you give out compliments like they are sweets **COMMITTED:** you still wear your school blazer **SINCERE:** you bake heart-shaped cookies for the food bank
1946-47 OR **2006-07** **FIRE DOG**	**ADVENTUROUS:** you will try anything once, but you are yet to locate the dirty wash basket **LOYAL:** you will only wear big brands **FUNNY:** though after too much cheese your humour can get a bit dark
1982-83 **WATER DOG**	**FUN-LOVING:** you terrorise the cat daily **EFFICIENT:** you always carry a pack of tissues **POPULAR:** you take homemade brownies into work on your birthday

WHICH DOG ARE YOU?

Hello there dog, wag your tail this way, look below to find out which dog you are.

2 FEB 1946 - 21 JAN 1947.............................**FIRE DOG**
18 FEB 1958 - 7 FEB 1959 ....**EARTH DOG**
6 FEB 1970 - 26 JAN 1971 ....**METAL DOG**
25 JAN 1982 - 12 FEB 1983.....................**WATER DOG**
10 FEB 1994 - 30 JAN 1995.....................**WOOD DOG**
29 JAN 2006 - 17 FEB 2007........................**FIRE DOG**
16 FEB 2018 - 4 FEB 2019 ....**EARTH DOG**
3 FEB 2030 - 22 JAN 2031 ....**METAL DOG**

WOOD DOG...GOOD DOG

You will always do what you say you will and will never leave a debt outstanding. You complete your paper round even in thick snow, as you can't bear to think of old people not being able to do their crossword. You are a thoroughly decent type and don't like any type of injustice, but you have been known to bare your teeth in the face of oppression. You're not interested in material gain, but you are partial to furnishing your home with dusty trinkets.

FIRE DOG...LOVING AND GIVING

You are comfortable in your own skin, which is just as well as you don't shower nearly enough. You are a gentle soul with a generous nature and would share your last mint with someone that you care about. Your impulsive nature and risk taking can mean that you lose everything you have worked on, just because you didn't press save before heading off to graze the treat cupboard. If there is something precious around it is likely that you will knock it over and you are forever losing things (you still have your gloves on strings).

EARTH DOG...PRIVATE INVESTIGATOR

You are the most logical of the dogs. Whilst the others are dreaming, you are busy sniffing around to get to the bottom of things. You always know where to find the best bacon sandwich in town. You are opinionated, but also wise, so people will hear you out, except when you start talking about the rugby. Only you understand your sense of humour.

METAL DOG...THE INFLUENCER

You are intelligent but attention-seeking. You post what you had for breakfast, lunch and tea and every run you do, plus pictures of you baking cakes and loading the washing machine and then you wonder why no one picks up when you call. That said, you are loyal and talented...just stop barking about all the boring stuff. You always look and smell nice.

WATER DOG...RRRRROGUE

You are the type to give someone a box of chocolates and then eat them all. You are quick-tempered, but you get away with it as you are truly loving (a bit like child birth, all is quickly forgotten). Your restless nature means you need a walk twice a day. You buy clothes that are practical and comfortable, you won't be gracing the catwalk any time soon.

DOG IN LOVE

You will wait to get your paws on your perfect partner, your patience will pay off, WOOF. Let's just make sure you're definitely a dog?

YES

NO → → → → →

MALE DOG

↓

YOU ARE

CONSIDERATE you insist on buying birthday cards with the age on the front. **HONEST** happy to admit to leaving the toilet seat up. **STUBBORN** you refuse to put on the central heating.

↓

YOU SHOULD

↓

SNOG ➡ **TIGER**

You are a pair of idealists who will go to heaven and back.

MARRY ➡ **RAT**

You two are cute and furry and you're not bothered about the body hair. When you find each other, it is undying love forever.

AVOID ➡ **GOAT**

There's no rolling in the haystack for you two, sheep does not like to be rounded up.

→ → → Oops you are in the wrong place, but nice try, better luck next time

FEMALE DOG
↓
YOU ARE

INDEPENDENT no one is going to put you on a lead. **GENTLE** to a point, but you are no push over. **IDEALISTIC** you spent too much time at school daydreaming and messed up your end-of-year tests.

↓
YOU SHOULD
↓

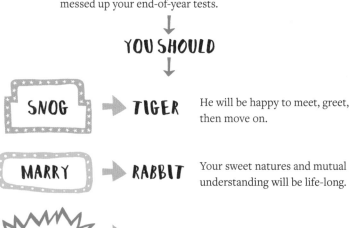

SNOG ➡ **TIGER**   He will be happy to meet, greet, then move on.

MARRY ➡ **RABBIT**   Your sweet natures and mutual understanding will be life-long.

AVOID ➡ **DRAGON**   Too much barking and hot air.

DOG AT WORK AND PLAY

DOG WORK

You are the best worker; loyal and hard-working, you won't stop until the job is done. You volunteer for everything and will always stay late to help out a colleague, especially if there's likely to be a pizza take-out in the offing. Sometimes you find yourself running round in circles, especially if there's a big decision to be made. You have to learn to back down graciously if you are barking up the wrong tree and must learn to manage your constant toilet breaks. You are very competitive; it isn't just about taking part for you and winning isn't everything, it's the only thing.

YOUR BEST JOBS

Gynaecologist

Autopsy technician

Priest

Judge

Pentathlete

Private investigator

Retail manager – home furnishings department

Stylist

YOUR BEST BUSINESS PARTNER

TIGER   A great pair, but you will do the donkey work when it comes to delivering.

RABBIT   You have mutual respect. A pair of people-pleasers, you're both good at digging yourself out of holes.

MONKEY   Creative and broadminded, you two could make a big impact.

PASTIMES AND HOBBIES

Whittling – you always find a good stick in the park

Theme parks – scream if you want to go faster

Mud runs (your mum's absolute favourite)

Allotment gardening – you are sorted if there's a food shortage

Eating with family and friends, you are always first to the table

HEALTH AND LIFESTYLE

You are always chasing after something – a school bus, a receipt that blew away in the wind...it's a good job that you have plenty of energy. Your downfall is your unhealthy diet, you are a secret sweet eater and you don't hide the wrappers very well. Secret anxieties can eat you up, but remember that no problem is so big that it can't be shared, but not on social media.

CELEBRITY DOGS

JUSTIN BIEBER
1 March 1994

Likes singing and tattoos, tries really hard to be bad.

MOTHER THERESA
26 August 1910

Marvellous woman, but had some bad habits.

DONALD TRUMP
14 June 1946

Built a load of naff hotels. Loose-lipped and loves playing top dog.

PRINCE WILLIAM
21 June 1982

Royal doggy at the beck and call of his granny – 'here boy'.

DAVID BOWIE
8 January 1947

Diamond dog. Aptly named.

JUDI DENCH
9 December 1934

Pretending to be a cat was not one of her better decisions.

ELEMENT	**WATER**
ENERGY	**YIN**
SEASON	**WINTER**
FLOWERS	**HYDRANGEA**
	DAISY
COLOURS	**YELLOW**
	GREY
	BROWN
	GOLD
STONE	**RUBY**
NAMES	**BABE**
	NAPOLEON
	WILBUR
	PERCY
	HUXLEY
	OLIVIA

PIG

22 JANUARY 1947 - 9 FEBRUARY 1948
8 FEBRUARY 1959 - 27 JANUARY 1960
27 JANUARY 1971 - 14 FEBRUARY 1972
13 FEBRUARY 1983 - 1 FEBRUARY 1984
31 JANUARY 1995 - 18 FEBRUARY 1996
18 FEBRUARY 2007 - 6 FEBRUARY 2008
5 FEBRUARY 2019 - 24 JANUARY 2020
23 JANUARY 2031 - 10 FEBRUARY 2032

YOUR PIG PERSONALITY

MALE

BORN IN	YOUR TRAITS
1959-60 OR **2019-20** EARTH PIG	**JUDICIOUS:** you know which bannisters to slide down and which to avoid **GENEROUS:** you share your sweets at bus stops **FRIENDLY:** you wave to anyone driving the same car as you
1971-72 OR **2031-32** METAL PIG	**AMBITIOUS:** you do mental maths in the shower **ORGANISED:** your sock drawer is in colour order **RELAXED:** you wear your loungewear to work on Fridays
1995-96 WOOD PIG	**HELPFUL:** you always volunteer to do match teas **CHATTY:** by the end of the day you have a sore throat **MODEST:** you don't tell people when you've completed the junior crossword
1947-48 OR **2007-08** FIRE PIG	**IMPATIENT:** you can't believe it's 300 days until Christmas **HARD-WORKING:** you've got to level 4625 of Candy Crush **RESPECTABLE:** you always wear deodorant
1983-84 WATER PIG	**DIPLOMATIC:** you always start an sentence with 'no offense but…' **TRUSTING:** you tend to get the wool pulled over your eyes **GOOD-HEARTED:** you phone your granny every Sunday without fail, even though she's at church

FEMALE

1959-60 OR **2019-20**
EARTH PIG

DIGNIFIED: you are like a swan but paddling slowly
BRAVE: you try not to cry when a plaster is ripped off
SENSIBLE: you wear flat shoes when you go out dancing

1971-72 OR **2031-32**
METAL PIG

OPEN: you insist on discussing what's in your packed lunch
CAREER-MINDED: you go to work on your birthday
STRONG: you can arm wrestle an ox, no problem

1995-96
WOOD PIG

DEMANDING: don't ask, don't get
CHEERFUL: rain is good for the plants
ENERGETIC: you always choose to take the stairs

1947-48 OR **2007-08**
FIRE PIG

QUIET: you are screaming on the inside
DECISIVE: if in doubt, you can't go wrong with black
QUICK-TEMPERED: wet towels on the floor drive you mad

1983-84
WATER PIG

STRONG-WILLED: otherwise known as plain naughty
CAREFUL: you never tread on the cracks
WISE: you buy a nine pack of toilet rolls to save money

WHICH PIG ARE YOU?

Hey this little piggy. No wandering off to market, just stay home and check out which sort of pig you are, there are so many lovely piggies that you could be... please refer below.

WOULD YOU MIND USING LESS SINGLE-USE PLASTIC, THANKS

22 JAN 1947 - 9 FEB 1948	**FIRE PIG**
8 FEB 1959 - 27 JAN 1960	**EARTH PIG**
27 JAN 1971 - 14 FEB 1972	**METAL PIG**
13 FEB 1983 - 1 FEB 1984	**WATER PIG**
31 JAN 1995 - 18 FEB 1996	**WOOD PIG**
18 FEB 2007 - 6 FEB 2008	**FIRE PIG**
5 FEB 2019 - 24 JAN 2020	**EARTH PIG**
23 JAN 2031 - 10 FEB 2032	**METAL PIG**

WOOD PIG...OVERLY NICE

You're like a pig in potato peelings when it's karaoke night down at your local – anything to spread the love and make friends and family happy. You are the type to put your food on other people's plates even when they don't want to try it (your insistence can be annoying). That said, you have a kind heart and a good snout for detail –the perfect companion on an orienteering trip, just don't be too pig-headed about which path to take.

FIRE PIG...SNOUT TO THE GROUND

You are the type to call a spade a spade; pretty handy when it comes to digging the garden. Undaunted by all that life can chuck at you, you are happiest when in a crowd at a concert or protest march (though you always make your point politely). You are always busy being busy and with hard work and ambition that is likely to pay off; you'll be able to afford a week in Tenerife once a year.

EARTH PIG...THIS LITTLE PIGGY STAYS AT HOME

You are happiest snuggled on the sofa with the dog. This is all very well as long as you avoid the shopping channels, as you can't resist the lure of a handy household item that can be paid for in instalments. But you are peaceful and lovable. So what if you don't have any money, you have the dog to keep you warm and happy.

METAL PIG...THE IN-HOUSE ARTIST

You have a great sense of purpose and always put your best trotter forward, but you sometimes struggle with making decisions...should you have a Mint Choc Chip or Raspberry Ripple cone? The creative in you will mean that you'll probably go for both and stick a flake and sauce on top. You can be a bit moody if someone takes a lick, and especially if they bite your flake.

WATER PIG...TOO LOVELY FOR WORDS

You are a piggy with an absolute heart of gold, you always look for the best in others, even if they have just nicked your wallet. You will just be upset that you can't get the first round in, but still you will look on the bright side and enjoy the company of others without a drink; it's not the end of the world.

PIG IN LOVE

Bless your little trotters, step this way to find your perfect partner. Firstly, just checking, you're a pig...

YES

NO → → → → →

MALE PIG

YOU ARE

GENTLE you are rubbish at massages and backscratching. **ATTENTIVE** you wipe any muck from your partner's face using a licked hanky. **WELL-MANNERED** you always hold the door open.

YOU SHOULD

SNOG → **TIGER** You make each other melt with desire.

MARRY → **RABBIT** You two are too sweet. You always agree with each other and wear matching outfits.

AVOID → **OX** You would grate on each other.

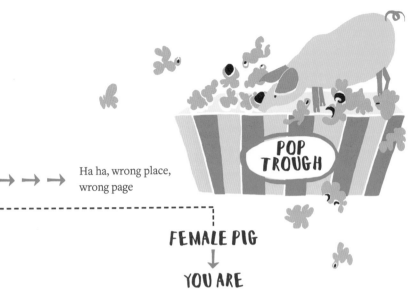

POP TROUGH

→ → → Ha ha, wrong place, wrong page

FEMALE PIG

↓

YOU ARE

CONSIDERATE you order for both of you. **INDEPENDENT** you will happily go to the cinema by yourself (you get more popcorn). **ROMANTIC** you compose naff poetry.

↓

YOU SHOULD

↓

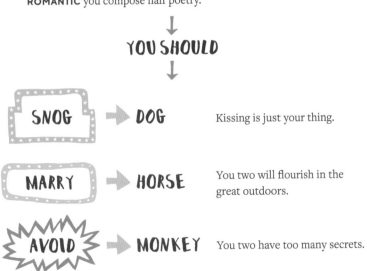

SNOG ➡ **DOG**   Kissing is just your thing.

MARRY ➡ **HORSE**   You two will flourish in the great outdoors.

AVOID ➡ **MONKEY**   You two have too many secrets.

PIG AT WORK AND PLAY

PIG WORK

Contrary to the belief that you are a grubby animal, you are clean, neat and well organised and, because of this, you are often put in charge of the stationery cupboard at work. Your thirst for knowledge and attention to detail make you a great team player. You can turn your hand to anything and are cooperative and flexible. Your happy demeanor will make any workplace a brighter place, but be careful not to annoy your colleagues by eating all the Christmas chocolates.

For you its all about taking part, unless there's a chocolate prize to be won.

YOUR BEST JOBS

Pastry chef

Clown

Cruise ship entertainer

Food writer

Nuclear scientist

Primary teacher

Caricature artist

Swede farmer

YOUR BEST BUSINESS PARTNER

TIGER The go-getter, tiger will seal the deal and then you can deliver it.

RABBIT An amiable meeting of minds that will get the job done nicely.

GOAT A trustworthy pair – shared values and good workers.

PASTIMES AND HOBBIES

Mud wrestling – get down and dirty

Apple bobbing (you love an apple, especially a Golden Delicious)

Slot machines (your dirty secret)

Entertaining – you are the High Host/ess

Wine tasting, or necking, in your case

Baking bread, if there's any flour in the house

Detectorist – you have a collection of beer bottle tops

HEALTH AND LIFESTYLE

Your love of all the good things in life can mean a robust waistline and dodgy heart. Stop hiding behind excuses and get yourself out for the Saturday morning Park Run. Fresh air, more apples and less wine will do you good. Don't ignore symptoms and make sure to drink plenty of fluids and you should have a good long life, but might need to go to the toilet more often than most.

CELEBRITY PIGS

CALVIN HARRIS
17 January 1984

Rich, handsome and musically-minded piggy.

HILARY CLINTON
26 October 1947

Thinks she looks good in a pant suit, debatable.

JACKSON POLLOCK
28 January 1912

Always the one who mixed up the paints at nursery.

HENRY FORD
30 July 1863

Good set of wheels on him.

KENDALL JENNER
3 November 1995

Trying to keep up with the rest of her family's antics is exhausting.

DUA LIPA
22 August 1995

She could be the one.